Game-Changing Strategies

Game-Changing Strategies

How to Create New Market Space in Established Industries by Breaking the Rules

Constantinos C. Markides

JOSSEY-BASS
A Wiley Imprint
www.josseybass.com

Published by Jossey-Bass
A Wiley Imprint
989 Market Street, San Francisco, CA 94103-1741—www.josseybass.com

Readers should be aware that Internet Web sites offered as citations and/or sources for further information may have changed or disappeared between the time this was written and when it is read.

Jossey-Bass books and products are available through most bookstores. To contact Jossey-Bass directly call our Customer Care Department within the U.S. at 800-956-7739, outside the U.S. at 317-572-3986, or fax 317-572-4002.

Jossey-Bass also publishes its books in a variety of electronic formats. Some content that appears in print may not be available in electronic books.

Library of Congress Cataloging-in-Publication Data

Markides, Constantinos.
    Game-changing strategies : how to create new market space in established industries by breaking the rules / Constantinos C. Markides. — 1st ed.
        p. cm.
    Includes bibliographical references and index.
    ISBN 978-0-470-27687-7 (cloth)
      1. Creative ability in business. 2. Organizational change. 3. Corporations—Growth. I. Title.
    HD53.M364 2008
    658.4'012—dc22

                                                                    2008009622

Printed in the United States of America
FIRST EDITION
HB Printing   10 9 8 7 6 5 4 3 2

Contents

To the memory of my friend and colleague,
Professor Paul Geroski

Introduction

Common sense as well as academic research argues that attacking bigger competitors will most likely lead to failure. For example, a series of studies undertaken at London Business School in the early 1990s examined how new market entrants in several U.K. industries fared against much bigger established competitors.[1] Not surprisingly, the failure rate of new entrants was quite high—more than 85 percent of them failed within five years of entry. The established competitors had few difficulties repelling these smaller attackers: the studies found that the top-ranked firm in a particular industry had a probability of about 96 percent of surviving as No. 1—a near certainty.[2] For the second-ranked firm the probability of survival was 91 percent, and for the third-ranked firm 80 percent. In fact, most of the turnover that occurred among the top five in an industry was due to mergers rather than smaller entrants outcompeting market leaders.

Yet, without disputing the statistics, we all know of examples of companies that attacked much bigger competitors with great success. In several instances, not only did the smaller firm survive, it managed to emerge as one of the leaders in the industry! IKEA did it in the furniture retail business, Canon in copiers, Bright Horizons in the child care and early education market, MinuteClinic in the general health care industry, Starbucks in coffee, Amazon in bookselling, K-Mart in retailing, Southwest, easyJet, and Ryanair in the airline industry, Red Bull in the carbonated soft drinks industry, Lulu in publishing, Enterprise in the car rental market, Netflix and Lovefilm in the DVD rental market, Honda in motorcycles, Wit Capital in investment banking, Skype in telephony, Priceline in the travel agent market, Casella in the wine market, Metro International in newspapers, and Home Depot in the home improvement market. The list could go on!

The Secret of Success: A New Business Model

What explains the success of these outliers and what can we all learn from their experiences? After studying more than seventy such firms, I believe that the answer to this question is simple enough: successful attackers do not try to be better than their bigger rivals. Rather, *they actively adopt a different strategy* (or business model) and aim to compete by changing the rules of the game in the industry. Over and over, what I have observed is that significant shifts in market share and company fortunes

---

Examples of Business-Model Innovators

The Body Shop	University of Phoenix
Amazon	Skype
Charles Schwab	Bright Horizons
Swatch	Metro International
Starbucks	Home Depot
IKEA	Bloomberg
Dell	eBay
Southwest and easyJet	Sephora
Kresge (K-Mart)	Travelocity
CNN	Priceline
Lulu	Akimbo
Nucor	Netflix and Lovefilm
MinuteClinic	ING Direct
Canon	LibraryThing

took place not by trying to play the game better than the competition but by playing a different game—in a sense, by avoiding head-on competition. The box lists a number of such business-model innovators from a variety of industries—both high-tech and low-tech, growing and mature.

Consider, for example, Enterprise Rent-A-Car, the biggest car rental company in North America. Rather than target travelers as its customers (as Hertz and Avis did), Enterprise focused on the replacement market (that is, providing cars to customers who'd had an accident). Rather than operate out of airports, it located its offices in downtown areas. Rather than use travel agents to push its services to end consumers, it uses insurance companies and auto mechanics. Rather than wait for the customer to pick up the rental, it brings the customer to the car. In short, Enterprise built a business model that is fundamentally different from those of its biggest competitors. This allowed it to start out in 1957 as a new start-up firm in the industry and grow into the biggest competitor in less than fifty years.

Consider also the case of MinuteClinic, a company founded in 2000 and already an industry leader in the retail-based health clinic industry in the United States. The company is based on the premise that certain simple health problems can be more quickly and cheaply diagnosed and treated at a walk-in clinic than in a doctor's office or an emergency room. Unlike traditional clinics that treat a wide variety of health problems, the company treats only common ailments such as strep throat and ear infections. It employs nurse practitioners armed with software that helps them test for and treat a handful of medical conditions. The software has the most up-to-date medical guidelines for diagnosis and treatment and applies strict rules that help ensure consistency of service. A doctor is generally available for phone consultation only. Prices are posted for all to see. Patients who come in with complaints not on the list or symptoms that indicate something more serious are referred to a doctor or an emergency room without a fee. The service does not require an appointment; it is quick

xii GAME-CHANGING STRATEGIES

(about fifteen minutes from start to finish), and it is cheap—a visit to test for strep throat costs $44 versus an average of $109 at a doctor's office or $328 in an emergency room.

Both examples highlight a generalization at the heart of this book: without the benefit of a technological innovation, it is extremely difficult for any firm to successfully attack bigger competitors or to successfully enter new markets where big established players rule. The strategy that seems to improve the *probability* of success in these situations is the strategy of breaking the rules—of discovering and exploiting a different business model from the one that the current leaders employ in a given industry.

So What?

Obviously this is not the first book to proclaim the virtues of this kind of innovation, and this is not the first time that managers have been encouraged to seek and exploit a new business model in their industry. Numerous books have been written and many ideas have been proposed on how firms could innovate in this way. For example, Kim and Mauborgne (2005) developed the beautiful concept of "blue ocean strategy" and formulated a number of analytical techniques (such as the "Strategy Canvas" and the concept of the "Value Curve") to help companies identify ways in which they can create new market space for themselves through business model innovation. Similarly, Christensen (1997) and Christensen and Raynor (2003) developed the concept of "disruptive innovation" and then used it to advise companies on how to develop new growth businesses using disruptive innovation as a platform.

Other authors have proposed even more radical ideas. For example, Hamel (1996, 1999, and 2000) proposed ideas such as making the strategy process democratic and bringing Silicon Valley inside the organization as ingredients to business-model innovation. Markides (1997, 1998) argued that corporations could learn from the success of the capitalist system by importing into their organizations those features of capitalism (such as decentralized allocation of resources and experimentation) that promote innovation. And Markides and Geroski (2005) suggested that big firms should help start-up firms create new business models and then use a "fast-second" strategy to acquire the start-up firms and scale up the new ways of competing. In short, the list of ideas on how to discover new business models is rather long; interested readers are also referred to the work of Charitou (2001), Gilbert (2003), Gilbert and Bower (2002), Hammer (2004), Kuhn and Marsick (2005), Mitchell and Coles (2003), and Slywotzky (1996).

But here's the catch—and the reason this book has come about. Despite all the advice and despite the wealth of ideas, it is very rare to find a business-model innovation that originated from an *established* big company. According to the available evidence:

- The majority of business-model innovations are introduced by newcomers in an industry (rather than established competitors).
- Not only do established competitors find it difficult to innovate in this manner, they also find it next to impossible to respond to such innovations in an effective way.
- Most of the time, the established firms' response is to imitate the innovation (rather than consider ways of neutralizing it or even destroying it).
- The majority of the responses fail because the established firms find it difficult to manage two different and conflicting games at the same time.

Why—despite all the ideas and advice—do big, established firms fail to pioneer new business models in their industries? These firms have the resources, the skills, and the technologies to do a much better job at innovation than the new start-up firms. Furthermore, the advice that has come their way on how to do so is good advice coming from some of the best academic minds. Yet they continue to allow new firms to take the initiative when it comes to business-model innovation, despite the obvious benefits of this type of innovation. What can explain this?

Creativity Is Not Enough

The purpose of this book is partly to explain the reasons behind this puzzle but mainly to use the insights from that explanation to develop practical ideas on how established companies could not only discover new, game-changing business models but also implement them next to their existing business models. As it turns out, all business-model innovations display certain characteristics that make them particularly unattractive to established firms. This suggests that giving more and better advice to established firms on how to become more creative so as to *discover* new business models is pointless. The issue is not discovery. The real issue is organizational, and the only advice that can prove helpful to established firms is how to overcome the organizational obstacles that hamper the implementation of new business models. This is exactly the emphasis of this book—not on discovering new business models but on implementing them.

At the same time, it should be obvious to all that despite all of the wonderful advice to the contrary, most new business models will be introduced by newcomers rather than by established firms. This is not because the established firms are stupid or bad at innovation. Rather, it's a reflection of how many companies inhabit an industry at any given time compared to how many potential entrants could invade that industry. For every established company trying to develop a new business model, there may be thousands of entrepreneurs attempting to do the same thing. Simple probability theory indicates that the chance that it will be a new entrant that discovers the new business model is much higher than the chance that it's going to be an established firm.

What this implies is that in addition to telling firms how to innovate, perhaps we also need to tell them how to respond if somebody else introduces a business-model innovation in their industry. This is another differentiating characteristic of this book—rather than dealing only with how firms can develop new game-changing business models in their industries, it also explores how firms can respond to this kind of innovation. Just as new entrants have advantages over the big firms when it comes to generating new business models, so do established firms have advantages over new entrants when it comes to responding to these invasions. The book will explore this theme.

This book has a third differentiating element. Over and above the fact that business-model innovation is an interesting phenomenon that deserves careful treatment, and over and above the fact that this kind of innovation is different from all other kinds of innovation, another major motivation behind this book is the desire to clarify a number of misconceptions and mistaken beliefs that have developed in the last few years about business-model innovation.

As I explain in the first chapter, business-model innovations tend to be disruptive to established firms for a number of reasons. As a result, many people have equated business-model innovation with disruptive innovation, as defined by Christensen (1997). This is a mistake. In his original formulation, Christensen focused primarily on technological innovation and explored how new technologies came to surpass seemingly "superior" technologies in a market. Over time, he widened the applicability of the term to include not only technologies but also products and business models. For example, Christensen and Raynor (2003) list as disruptive innovations such disparate things as discount department stores; low-price, point-to-point airlines; cheap, mass-market products such as power tools, copiers, and motorcycles; and online businesses such as bookselling, education, brokerage, and travel arrangements.

Although I agree that all these innovations are "disruptive" to incumbents, treating them all as one and the same has actually confused matters considerably. This is because a disruptive technological innovation is a fundamentally different phenomenon from a disruptive business-model innovation or a disruptive product innovation—these innovations arise in different ways, have different competitive effects, and require different responses from incumbents. Lumping all types of disruptive innovation into one category simply mixes apples with oranges.

This confusion can be seen more clearly if you compare the effect on incumbents of disruptive *technological* innovations to the effect of disruptive *business-model* innovations. A key finding in Christensen's work is that disruptive technological innovations eventually grow to dominate the market. Christensen and Raynor (2003, p. 69) make this point forcefully by arguing, "Disruption is a process and not an event. . . . It might take decades for the forces to work their way through an industry but [they] are always at work." Similarly, Danneels (2004) summarizes the existing theory on disruptive innovation by pointing out that "disruptive technologies tend to be associated with the replacement of incumbents by entrants." If correct, such a "fact" carries a serious implication for incumbent firms—namely that the only way to respond to the disruption is to accept it and then find ways to exploit it. Christensen and Raynor suggest that established companies could exploit a disruption only by creating a separate unit.

Yet, as I argue in this book, the evidence on business-model innovation does not support such an extreme position. What often happens in the case of a business-model innovation is that the new way of competing in the business grows (usually quickly) to a certain percentage of the market but fails to completely overtake the traditional way of competing. For example, Internet banks and Internet brokerage firms have grown rapidly in the last five years but have captured only 10 percent to 20 percent of the market. Similarly, budget, no-frills flying as a way of business has grown phenomenally since 1995 but has captured no more than 20 percent of the total market. In market after market, the new ways of playing the game grow to a respectable size but never really replace the old ways. Nor are these innovations expected to grow in the future to 100 percent of their markets.

If that is the case when it comes to business-model innovation, then some of the "accepted wisdom" on disruptive business-model innovation needs to be modified. First, new business models are not necessarily superior to the ones established companies employ. This implies that it is not necessarily an optimal strategy for an established company to abandon its existing business model in favor of something new or to grow the new business model alongside its existing business model. The decision should be based on a careful cost-benefit analysis of the specific circumstances of the firm as well as on the nature of the innovation.

The truth of the matter is that established companies simply find most business-model innovations unattractive. This is not for the reasons articulated in Christensen (1997)—though these reasons undoubtedly play a role. Rather, most business-model innovations simply do not make economic sense for established companies. In its efforts to grow, the established firm has many other alternatives to consider—including investing its limited resources in adjacent markets or taking its existing business model internationally. Given its other growth options (and given its limited resources), the decision to invest in the disruption may rank low on a firm's priority list. In any case, the decision to invest in a new business model is not (and should not be) an automatic one.

A second sacred cow about disruptive innovations is that the best way for an established company to adopt and exploit such innovations is through a separate unit. Presumably, this is the best way to overcome the inherent conflicts between the established business and the innovation. Yet as I explain in Chapters Four and Five, established companies could exploit disruptive business-model innovations in a number of ways—and they don't necessarily have to use a separate unit to do so.

Finally, even if the disruptive innovation is not superior to the established business model, incumbents need to find a way to respond to it. However, this does not necessarily mean that they have to adopt every innovation that comes along. They could respond to an innovation not by adopting it but by investing in their existing business to make the traditional way of competing even more competitive relative to the new way of competing. They even have the option of counterattacking the innovators by trying to "disrupt the disruptors."

Thus, to summarize what I have argued so far: this book emphasizes the implementation of new business models rather than their discovery. It tackles not only the issue of introducing new business models but also that of responding to them, and it dispels a few misconceptions about this type of innovation along the way. Whether all this justifies the writing (or reading) of yet another book on innovation is for the reader to decide. Suffice it to say that the content of this book represents the summary of more than fifteen articles and chapters on this topic that I have published over the past ten years.

A Very Specific Type of Innovation

It is important to stress from the very beginning that what I say in this book applies only to a very specific type of innovation—the discovery and exploitation of a game-changing strategy (or business model). I want to alert the reader to this simple point because it has become common lately for all of us to talk about innovation in general as if all types of innovations are one and the same. Nothing could be further from the truth. Business-model innovation is not the same thing as product innovation.

And it is certainly different from technological innovation. Treating them as one and the same is misleading.

Every company wants to achieve growth and profitability; what better way to do so than by creating totally new market space through innovation? Who wants to get messy and bloodied by fighting battles for market share with aggressive competitors in existing markets when there's virgin territory to discover and colonize? Therefore, discovering (or creating) new market space (that is, innovation!) should be the goal and ambition of every company.

While this is obvious and noncontroversial, the devil is always in the detail. For example, what exactly does the phrase "create new market space through innovation" mean? As we all know, there are different types of innovation with different competitive effects, each one capable of producing huge new markets. Which of these should a company then pursue to create new market space? And are the prerequisites for achieving one type of innovation the same as those for achieving another type of innovation?

New markets could be created in a variety of ways. For example, Apple, 3M, and Nestlé created new market space by discovering the iPod, Post-It note, and Nespresso, respectively. This is what we traditionally call product innovation. On the other hand, Enterprise Rent-A-Car created the huge replacement market in the car rental industry without even introducing a new product—instead, it creatively segmented the market in a new way. Similarly, Schwab and Amazon created new market space by using the Internet to grow online brokerage and bookselling, respectively—this is what is now called business-model innovation. And Canon, Honda, and P&G did it by using innovative strategies to scale up existing product niches—the copier, motorcycle, and disposable diaper markets, respectively—and convert them into mass markets.

All these companies employed innovation to create new market space, but the type of innovation that Apple used is fundamentally different from the type of innovation that Enterprise used. The point is that *innovation* is not one thing. It comes in different types—product, technological, business model, and so on—all of which are capable of creating new market space. And it should come as no surprise to hear that what a company needs to do to achieve one type of innovation is totally different from what it must do to achieve another type of innovation. This implies that simply asking, "How can I make my company more innovative?" does *not* make sense! A useful prescription cannot be given without first specifying what specific type of innovation a company aspires to achieve.

Imagine going to the doctor because you don't feel well. How would you react if the doctor prescribes a medicine without first identifying what you are suffering from? It sounds silly, yet this is exactly what most of us do when it comes to prescribing advice to companies on "how to become more innovative." Given the number of different types of innovation that a company could aspire to achieve, prescribing the same "medicine" for all is like taking the same medicine for whatever disease one has!

Business-model innovation is unique in that it has certain characteristics, gets created in a certain way, grows in specific ways, and displays certain attributes that make it very difficult for big, established companies to create or grow. To fully appreciate why this kind of innovation presents such an enormous challenge for established firms, it is necessary to first understand its unique way of entering established markets, its unique way of growing, and the features that characterize it. Only then can we offer meaningful and useful advice on how established firms could exploit this kind of innovation.

Like technological and product innovations, business-model innovations can also create huge new markets. For example, the next table lists a number of markets that have been created through innovation—those on the left came about through radical product innovation while those on the right came about through business-model innovation. Both types of markets are important, but the innovation process that created those on the left is fundamentally different from the innovation process that created those on the right. By implication, the "medicine" that a company needs to take to achieve business-model innovation is different from the medicine that it needs for radical product innovation. Our objective in this book is to explore how companies achieve business-model innovation and create new markets on the periphery of their existing markets.

New Markets Created Through Innovation

New Markets Created Through Radical Product Innovation	New Markets Created Through Business-Model Innovation
Television	Internet banking
Personal computers	Low-cost, point-to-point flying
Personal digital assistants (PDAs)	Private label consumer goods
Cars	Screen-based electronic trading systems
Supercomputers	Generic drugs
Semiconductors	Online distribution of groceries
Mobile phones	Catalog retailing
Video cassette recorders (VCRs)	Department stores
Medical diagnostic imaging	Steel minimills
Computer operating systems	Online universities

The Structure of the Book

To appreciate why business-model innovation is so difficult for most firms to achieve, Chapter One provides a precise definition of this phenomenon and describes its main characteristics. Specifically, business-model innovation is defined as the discovery of a different business model in an existing industry. If successful, new business models enlarge the overall market by attracting non-consumers into the market or by encouraging existing consumers to consume more. Thus they can be the source of tremendous growth for a firm.

This point is so important that it needs reemphasizing. Other researchers have pointed out that the discovery of a new, game-changing business model could prove very profitable for a firm. Yet the real reasons behind its profitability are not fully appreciated. Yes, it is true that the new business model is so unorthodox that it confuses competitors and constrains them from responding quickly or aggressively enough. It's also true that the new business model conflicts with the existing business models in the industry and this prevents established competitors from reacting aggressively. However, the main factor behind the profitability of this kind of innovation is that it enlarges the market. It does so either by attracting new consumers into the market (like Southwest and easyJet) or by encouraging existing ones to consume more (like Amazon). I will say more about this in the next chapter but for the time being suffice it to say that business-model innovation can be very profitable for the innovators.

However, new business models invade existing markets by offering different value propositions from what the established players are offering. As a result, they attract different customers from the ones who go to the established firms. To serve these different customers, the innovators need to develop a business system that is not only different but also conflicts with the business systems used by the established players. All this means that established firms would find these kinds of innovations extremely unpalatable and would have few incentives to pursue them.

This point needs to be appreciated because it implies that it is not enough to simply proclaim the virtues of business-model innovations and expect established firms to "just do it." It's only when the firm puts in place organizational structures that make the new business model less conflicting and more palatable to the existing business that it makes sense to actively pursue this kind of innovation. Therefore, the task must be to explore what these organizational solutions are.

I do so in Chapters Two through Five. First, Chapter Two examines how established firms discover new business models. This is all about enhancing corporate creativity, and numerous other books have explored this topic. My emphasis, therefore, is not so much on the analytical techniques that a firm could use to dream up innovative new business models as on the organizational constraints that prevent established firms from becoming creative. Specifically, I propose that a prerequisite to creativity is a fundamental questioning of the firm's existing business model. However, real questioning will take place in a firm only after a *positive crisis* has been created. I explain what this is and how to create one.

But discovering new business models is the easy part! One of the most difficult aspects of business-model innovation is to implement such radical strategies in the marketplace so as to deliver real value to customers in a cost-efficient and profitable way. Chapter Three argues that information and communication technology (ICT) is a key enabler in the successful implementation of radical new strategies. Specifically, I show that ICT enables firms to reach consumers that most competitors cannot serve profitably, offer radically new value propositions to consumers that other firms cannot deliver in a cost-efficient way, and put in place value chains that no other firm could do efficiently. ICT also allows business-model innovators to scale up their business models quickly and so protect themselves from competitive attacks.

Another key problem for established companies is how to manage a new business model next to their current one. According to existing academic theories, the challenge with attempting to manage two different business models in the same market is that the two models (and their underlying value chains) would conflict with one another. The existence of trade-offs and conflicts means that a company that tries to compete in both positions simultaneously risks paying a huge straddling cost and degrading the value of its existing activities (Porter, 1996).

The primary solution offered in the literature on how to solve this problem is to keep the two business models (and their underlying value chains) physically separate in two distinct organizations. This is the "innovator's solution" that's primarily associated with Clayton Christensen's work on disruptive innovation. Chapter Four challenges this view and proposes a contingency approach to the dilemma. I argue that there are circumstances when the firm needs to create a separate unit for the new business model, but there are also circumstances when such a separate unit is not necessary. The trick is to balance the benefits of keeping the two business models separate while at the same time integrating them enough so as to allow them to exploit synergies with one another. The chapter describes four possible strategies that companies could use to achieve such a balance.

Simply deciding when to separate and when to keep a new business model inside the existing organization is only part of the solution. Some companies separated their new business model and were successful (Singapore Airlines), but other companies did the same thing and were unsuccessful (Continental Airlines). Similarly, some companies did not create a separate unit for their new business model (that is, they kept it integrated in the existing organization) and succeeded (SMH and Swatch) while other companies (such as the Indian tractor manufacturer HMT International) did the same thing but failed . Therefore, having decided which of these strategies a firm will adopt (based on its own circumstances) the key question that must be addressed is: "What else do I need to do to make each strategy successful?" Chapter Five explores this issue and describes how established firms can achieve ambidexterity.

Of course, in the majority of cases, it is not the incumbents that pioneer the new business models but the founders of new start-up firms. In such cases, the issue for incumbents is how to respond to the invading business model. But, as noted earlier, this response does not necessarily involve adopting the new business model; they can improve their current business model or use it to disrupt the innovators. Chapter Six explores the various response options available to established firms and discusses when a firm should do what.

The discussion in the first six chapters has assumed that the established firm is pursuing a new, game-changing strategy in its own industry. However, it is important to appreciate that business-model innovation could also take place in markets that differ from the established firm's main market. In fact, the use of a radical new business model becomes an absolute necessity for any firm in at least two instances, both of which involve a different market from the firm's main business:

- Entering another established market, in effect attacking entrenched competitors in that market
- Scaling up a new market that is in its early formative years

In both these instances, the established firm will have the proper incentives to pioneer a business-model innovation. Chapter Seven explores these instances in more detail.

Finally, Chapter Eight tries to bring everything together by proposing that even though business-model innovation is difficult for established firms, they still have to be proactive about it rather than simply respond to it. The chapter explains how they could do so and proposes a solution that encourages established firms to treat business-model innovation differently from all other types of innovations they may be promoting.

Game-Changing Strategies

1

THE INNOVATION IS IN THE BUSINESS MODEL

When Roger and Linda Mason decided to start a child-care company in 1987, they couldn't have chosen a less attractive industry! The child-care industry in the United States was run as a commodity business, characterized by low margins, no barriers to entry, few economies of scale, massive labor intensity, and no brand distinction. Yet the Masons succeeded in building their new company—Bright Horizons—into the world's leading provider of employer-sponsored child care, early education, and work-life solutions, operating more than six hundred centers for the world's leading employers in the United States, Europe, and Canada. Plus, they did all this while delivering high returns—on average, a 50 percent return on invested capital per center. How did they do it?

The secret of their success lies in the business model that they developed to compete in this market.[1] Rather than target parents as prospective customers (as all other child-care centers did), Bright Horizons's founders focused on employers. Rather than build their own centers at locations of their choosing, they formed partnerships with employers who financed the building of centers on their premises. Rather than compete on cost, they differentiated themselves on quality. Rather than pay their teachers an average salary to control their costs, they offered 20–30 percent above average compensation along with comprehensive benefits. And rather than offer a standardized curriculum in every center, they customized the centers so that their design, hours of operation, and age-group configuration matched the requirements and needs of their clients. In short, Bright Horizons built and exploited a business model in the day-care industry that was fundamentally different from the business model that the established competitors were using.

Note that Bright Horizons did not discover a new product— what they offer is still child-care services, very much like all other competitors in this market. But they do so in a fundamentally different way and to a fundamentally different customer from the one all other competitors address. In other words, Bright Horizons innovated in its market, but the innovation is not in discovering new products or technologies—it is in discovering a new *business model*.

Numerous other companies that innovated in this manner spring to mind. For example, when Jeff Bezos founded Amazon in 1995, he introduced a new business model in the book retailing business that was manifestly different from the business model that traditional players like Borders and Barnes & Noble employed at the time. Similarly, companies such as Charles Schwab, easyJet, IKEA, Netflix, Home Depot, and Dell are all examples of innovators who attacked their competitors in their respective industries not by introducing new products or tech-nologies but by applying different business models. New business models have been invading existing markets with increasing fre-quency, and Table 1.1 lists just a few of the industries that have been affected. Appendix A at the end of the book describes the stories of some less well-known business-model innovators of the last twenty years.

What Is a Business Model?

What exactly is a business model? Different people have given dif-ferent answers to this question (for example, Casadesus-Masanell and Ricart, 2007; Hambrick and Fredrickson, 2001; Johnson and

Table 1.1. Examples of Business-Model Innovations.

Industry	New Business Model	Innovator(s) and Date of Introduction
General retailing (U.S.)	Online distribution • Books • Music	Amazon.com: • July 1995 • June 1998
Car rental industry (U.S.)	Focusing on a different type of customers, and operating an extensive network of car rental offices located in cities, rather than at major airports	Enterprise Rent-A-Car: 1957
Computer industry (U.S.)	Selling computers directly to customers	Dell Computer: 1983
Retail brokerage industry (U.S.)	Online trading	Aufhauser & Co.: 1994 E-Trade, Charles Schwab: 1996
Retail brokerage industry (U.S.)	Operating an extensive network of single-broker offices across the country as separate profit centers	Edward Jones & Co.: 1972 (when the company formally adopted the new business model)
Steel industry (U.S.)	Introduction of minimills (a low-cost production method to make flat-rolled sheet steel, a high-end steel product)	Nucor Corporation: 1969 (introduced the world's first continuous thin-slab casting facility for sheet steel)
Automobile industry (Europe)	Mass-customized cars	Smart car (by DaimlerChrysler): October 1998
Used car business (U.S.)	A new retail and distribution method for selling used cars (extensive refurbishing of cars, product guarantees, no-haggle pricing, and sophisticated use of in-house financing)	AutoNation USA, CarMax: 1996

(Continued)

Table 1.1.   (continued)

Industry	New Business Model	Innovator(s) and Date of Introduction
Banking industry (U.K.)	Direct banking • Telephone banking • PC banking • Online banking	First Direct: • October 1989 • May 1996 • Summer 1997
General insurance industry (U.K.)	Direct insurance • Direct motor insurance • Direct home insurance	Direct Line Insurance • April 1985 • Autumn 1993
Life insurance and pensions industry (U.K.)	Direct life insurance and personal pensions	Virgin Direct: June 1996
Airline industry (Europe)	Low-cost, no-frills, point-to-point airline service	Ryanair: 1991 (routes between U.K. and Ireland only) easyJet: November 1995
Retail supermarket industry (U.K.)	Home-delivery grocery service Online home-delivery grocery service	Food Ferry Co., Teleshop: Early 1990s (London area only) Tesco Direct: 1998 (now part of Tesco.com, launched in 2000)
Stock exchanges (Europe and North America)	Electronic communications networks (ECNs)	OM Exchange: 1984 (Recently, new ECNs such as Instinet, Island, and OptiMark were introduced in European and North American exchanges)

Suskewicz, 2007; Markides, 1997; Mitchell and Coles, 2003; Slywotzky, 1996; Slywotzky and Morrison, 2002; Voelpel, Leibold, Tekie, and Von Krogh, 2005). Consider just three of the definitions that have been provided in the business literature. Slywotzky (both independently and with Morrison) argued that a business model is made up of the decisions that a company makes on eleven dimensions:

- Fundamental assumptions about the business
- Customers selected
- Scope of activities
- Source of differentiation
- Value recapture
- Purchasing system
- Manufacturing system
- Capital intensity
- R&D and product development system
- Organizational configuration
- Go-to-market mechanism

On the other hand, Hambrick and Fredrickson identified five key elements that make up a business model:

- Where will we be active (and with how much emphasis)?
- How will we get there?
- How will we win?
- How will we obtain our returns?
- What will be our speed and sequence of moves?

And Mitchell and Coles (p. 3) provided a definition that includes six main elements, namely: "the who, what, when, where, why and how much a company uses to provide its goods and services and receive value for its efforts."

For the purposes of this book, I will use a simpler definition based on the pioneering work of Derek Abell (1980), who held that a business model is the sum of the answers that a company gives to these three interrelated questions:

- *Who* should I target as customers?
- *What* products or services should I be offering them and what should be my (differentiated) value proposition?
- *How* should I do this in an efficient way?

While I do not pretend that the definition adopted here is exhaustive or better than all the others proposed by other people, I do believe that it is adequate for the purposes of exploring business-model innovation.

The Who-What-How decisions define the parameters within which the company will operate. By definition, they also determine the terrain for which the company will *not* fight: the customers it will not pursue, the investments it will not finance, the competitors it will not respond to. As a result, these decisions are painful to make and are often preceded by internal arguments, disagreements, and politicking. But unless a decision is taken, the company will find itself spreading its limited resources too widely with no clear focus or direction.

The answers to the Who-What-How questions form the heart of the strategy of any company—in fact some will argue that the combined answer to these questions *is* the strategy of a company. One could enlarge this definition of strategy to incorporate the When-Where-Why questions as well, but the added complexity is not necessary to understand how and when companies pursue business-model innovation.

What Is an Innovation?

To qualify as an innovation, the new business model must not only be new to the innovating company but also *new to the world*. For this to happen, the new business model must be offering something that nobody else is currently offering. This might seem an unusually high hurdle to jump, but what it effectively means is that the innovation must not only steal market share from established competitors but *should also enlarge the existing economic pie*—either by attracting new customers into the market or by encouraging existing customers to consume more. In this sense, the innovation *creates value* rather than simply being a value transfer from one firm to another.

This implies that business-model innovation is much more than the discovery of a radical new strategy on the part of a firm. For example, IBM's change of strategy in the early 1990s, radical as it may have been, is not a business-model innovation. On the other hand, companies such as Amazon, Schwab, Dell, IKEA, Swatch, and Southwest are considered business-model innovators because they introduced new business models in their respective markets that attracted new consumers or got existing consumers to consume more (and so enlarged their markets).

It is important to note that business-model innovators do not discover new products or services—they simply redefine what an existing product or service is and how it is provided to the customer. For example, Amazon did not discover bookselling— it redefined what the service is all about, what the customer gets out of it, and how the service is provided to the customer. Similarly, Swatch did not discover the watch—it redefined what this product is and why the customer should buy it. In short, the innovation is in the discovery of a different business model (not product) in an existing industry.

Making an assessment whether a new business model is really different from an established one is, obviously, a very subjective exercise. Nevertheless, it is possible to measure the level of difference in a systematic way. For example, Table 1.2 uses the Slywotzky (1996) definition of a business model to list a number of questions that could be asked to assess whether a new business model in an industry is different to the existing one.

Table 1.2.   Competitive Dimensions for New Business Models.

Competitive Dimension	Key Questions
Fundamental assumptions	Compared to the existing business, does the new strategic position aim to satisfy a different set of customers' priorities? Are the profit drivers for the new business different from those of the existing business?
Customer selection	Compared to the existing business, does the new strategic position aim to serve a different type of customer?
Scope	Compared to the existing business, does the new strategic position involve a different product or service? Does the new position require a different set of activities?
Differentiation	Compared to the existing business, does the new strategic position have a different basis for differentiation? Is the value proposition for the new business different from that offered by incumbent firms in the existing business?
Manufacturing and operating system	Compared to the existing business, does the new strategic position involve a different kind of manufacturing or service delivery economics and methods?
Organizational configuration	Compared to the existing business, does the new strategic position involve a different organizational structure?
Go-to-market mechanism	Compared to the existing business, does the new strategic position use a different distribution method to deliver the products or services to the market?

Source: Adapted from Slywotzky, 1996.

Characteristics of Business-Model Innovations

All business-model innovations share certain common characteristics. They tend to invade existing industries in a very specific way, grow in a specific manner, and display characteristics that make them disruptive to established firms. To illustrate these points, here's an example.

The Online Brokerage Market

In 1996, online trading emerged as a new way of doing business in the U.S. retail brokerage industry.[2] Companies such as E-Trade, Charles Schwab, Ameritrade, and Fidelity were among the first to offer low-cost online trading to customers, thereby creating a new customer segment and a new way of competing in the industry. Since then, online trading in the United States has experienced dramatic growth. A study by Morgan Stanley Dean Witter estimated that online accounts would increase from 5.7 million (or 9 percent of total retail accounts) in 1998 to approximately 44 million online accounts (or 50 percent of total retail accounts) by 2003.[3] Several other studies have estimated that online trading now represents a multibillion-dollar industry that accounts for more than 50 percent of all retail trades.

Compared to traditional brokerage, online trading represented a fundamentally different way of competing in this business. Whereas full-service brokerage houses relied on an extensive network of brokers and branch offices to build relationships with customers, online traders relied on impersonal transactions to execute trades. And whereas traditional brokerage houses based their fees on the research and advice that they provided to customers, the online traders' value proposition was low price and speed of execution.

Even though revenues per trade were lower for Internet brokers, increased usage (investors traded more frequently once they were online) as well as lower operating costs made these online services potentially highly profitable. The online brokers' lower operating cost base was reflected in the low prices (commissions) that they charge. But they offered much more than just lower prices. Increasingly, online brokers provided clients with a broad range of investment research from third-party sources, enabling private investors to make objective decisions and take investment actions on their own. These services included access to real-time, personalized market information and financial data, news, company research, market analysis, and other investment information services. Moreover, online tools for tracking portfolio performance could also help investors manage their accounts without having to seek advice from a broker. Therefore, online brokers had radically redefined the existing rules of the game in the retail brokerage industry by giving customers access to information and research once available only to brokerage professionals.

Not only was this way of doing business radically different from the traditional way, it also raised thorny issues for any established competitor contemplating adoption of online trading. A potential trade-off that a full-service brokerage house was likely to face was cannibalization of its existing full-service customer base. By offering online services, the company risked shifting some of its more independent-minded private investors from high-value, advisory-based activities to low-margin, execution-only services offered through the Internet. These investors could come to consider trade execution as a commodity and could therefore opt to use the company's online site to trade directly rather than use the help and advice of brokers and pay traditional broker commissions.

In addition, if the established brokerage house chose to embrace the new online trading business, it faced the challenge of what to do with its existing branch network and brokers. Should it divert much-needed resources from its traditional business to the online business, thereby undermining the value of its existing distribution channel? The decision was not an easy one. The very act of setting up an online operation would not only create competition for resources between the alternative distribution channels but would also undermine one of the core advantages of the full-service firms, namely the broker's role in providing sound advice to clients. Such a strategy could very easily alienate the firm's brokers.

Thus, by adopting an altogether different business model, online brokers were challenging the traditional full-service business model and threatening the long-standing competitive positions of incumbent firms in this industry. Their unorthodox tactics made it difficult to find an appropriate response. The underlying trade-offs between the two different ways of competing in the industry added to this difficulty considerably, and made the decision on whether or not to offer online trading a major dilemma for the established firms.

Some Common Themes

Certain themes emerge from the online brokerage example that are actually common to all business-model innovations.

First, new business models invade an existing market by *emphasizing product or service attributes that are different from those emphasized by the traditional business models of the established competitors.* For example, whereas traditional brokers sell their services on the basis of their research and advice to customers, online brokers sell on the back of a different value proposition, namely price and speed of execution. Similarly, whereas traditional airline companies sell their product on the basis of frequency, range of destinations, and quality of service on board, the low-cost, point-to-point operators emphasize price. And whereas traditional universities sell their product on the basis of quality and career placement, online schools like the Open University in the United Kingdom and University of Phoenix in the United States sell their education on the basis of flexibility and price. This point is made vividly clear in Table 1.3, which compares the performance attributes emphasized by established firms to those emphasized by innovators in a number of industries.

This is an important point to appreciate. Since innovators emphasize different dimensions of a product or service, their

Table 1.3.   Critical Performance Attributes Emphasized by Established Firms and Innovators.

Industry	Performance Attributes Emphasized by Established Firms	Performance Attributes Emphasized by Business-Model Innovators
Banking	Extensive, nationwide branch network and personal service	24-hour access, convenience, price
Insurance	Personal, face-to-face advice through an extensive agent network	Convenience and low commission rates
Airlines	Hub-and-spoke system, premium service, meals, baggage checking	Price, no frills
Brokerage	Research and advice	Speed of execution and price
Photocopying	Speed of copying	Price, size, and quality
Watches	Accuracy and functionality	Design
Steel	Quality	Price
Motorcycles	Speed and power	Size and price
Bookstores	Chain of superstores offering nice environment and service	Wide selection, speed, price, convenience
Car rental	Location (airports) and quality of cars	Location (downtown) and price
Computer	Speed, memory capacity, power	Design and user-friendliness

products or services inevitably become attractive (at least originally) to a different customer base from the one that desires what the traditional competitors offer. As a result, the markets that get created around the new competitors tend to be composed of different customers and have different key success factors from the established competitors' markets.

This is a point that Christensen (1997) emphasizes in his own work on disruptive innovation. Based on his research, Christensen suggests that established players in an industry tend to focus on certain product or service attributes that their mainstream customers value. The established players invest aggressively to improve these performance attributes and thus retain their existing customers. In contrast, new companies enter the industry by emphasizing different product or service attributes. The newcomers bring to the market a very different value proposition from the one available previously. They typically offer different performance attributes from the ones mainstream customers historically valued and, at least at the outset, they almost always perform far worse along one or two dimensions that are particularly important to those customers. As a result, mainstream customers are usually unwilling to adopt these disruptive innovations since they do not meet their current needs.

This means that the innovation will succeed only if another set of customers—different from the mainstream customers—finds its offering attractive enough. In fact, this is exactly what happens. Even though the innovation generally underperforms mainstream products or services in the dimensions emphasized by the established players, it has other features and attributes that are superior to those of established firms and that a certain (and usually new) segment of customers values. The new customer segment becomes the platform from which the innovator will eventually grow and invade the mainstream customer base.

A second characteristic that all business-model innovations display is that they start out small relative to the main business. Often (but not always), they also start out as low-margin businesses. As a result, it is difficult to gain support or long-term commitment from the organization of the established competitors. Exactly because the innovations are so small relative to the mainstream business, they are not particularly attractive to big, established companies. Even managers in these established companies who want to do something about the new markets find it difficult to justify investment in these markets on economic grounds. As long as the incumbents are able to retain their mainstream customers in their existing business, they are unwilling to invest significant resources in the innovation. Not surprisingly, it is rare to find these types of innovations originating from big, established companies. It is usually an entrepreneur or a new market entrant that introduces business-model innovations in an existing market.

However, it is not long before the innovations start growing into viable businesses! This is the third characteristic common to all business-model innovations. The way this growth happens is also quite similar across industries and follows a predictable pattern.

Once innovators become established in their *new* (and small) segment, a series of improvements over time enhance not only their original value proposition but also the performance attributes that established companies emphasize (and mainstream customers value). In fact, these performance attributes improve at such a rapid rate that the innovators can soon enter the established market and sell their previously inferior product or service to the mainstream customers (Christensen, 1997). This is because they are able to deliver performance that is *good enough* in the old attributes (that established competitors emphasize) and *superior* in the new attributes. By accumulating experience and relevant expertise in the new market, the innovators can then use that commercial platform to attack the value networks of the established firms. In their constant effort to improve their products and services to beat the competition, these companies invest resources to the point where they can address the needs of mainstream customers. This is what ultimately leads to the growth of the innovation into a big business.

For example, consider again the U.S. retail brokerage industry. Online brokers such as Charles Schwab and E-Trade are now able to offer high-quality research and financial advice to their investors at much lower cost per trade compared to the established full-service brokerage houses. The online brokers offer access to real-time, personalized market information and financial data, market analysis, and other investment information services once provided only by traditional full-service companies. Similarly, Internet banks (such are First Direct in the United Kingdom) are now focusing on providing more customized personal services to their customers by expanding their range of products. In addition to offering online accounts, these banks are increasingly tailoring specific products for the Internet, like online billing or credit cards with instant online approval. They are also enhancing their level of service through online content by providing investment research and personal financial advice to customers, services that were previously available only through a retail branch network.

Inevitably, the growth of the innovator into the mainstream business attracts the attention of established players. As more customers (both existing and new ones) embrace the innovation, the new business receives increasing attention from both the media and the established players. A point is reached where established players cannot afford to ignore this new way of doing business and they therefore begin to consider ways to respond to it.

At this stage of deciding how to respond, established firms have to confront the fourth characteristic that all such innovations share: compared to the traditional business, the markets created by business-model innovations have different key success factors and as a result require a different combination of tailored activities on the part of the firm. For example, the value chain as well as the internal processes, structures, and cultures that Amazon needs to put in place to compete successfully in the online distribution of books is demonstrably different from the one that Borders or Barnes & Noble needs to compete in the same industry using their business model.

Not only are the new required activities different, they are often incompatible with a company's existing set of activities. This is because of various trade-offs or conflicts that exist between the two ways of doing business. For example, by selling its tickets through the Internet just like its low-cost competitors, British Airways risks alienating its existing distributors (the travel agents).

Similarly, if Unilever moves aggressively into lower-price private label brands, it risks damaging its existing brands and diluting the organization's strong culture for innovation and differentiation. The next box lists a few of the most serious conflicts and trade-offs that might exist between the new business model and the established one.

Potential Conflicts and Trade-offs Between the Established Business Model and the New One

- Risk of cannibalizing the existing customer base
- Risk of destroying or undermining the value of the existing distribution network
- Risk of compromising the quality of service offered to customers
- Risk of undermining the company's image or reputation and the value associated with it
- Risk of destroying the overall culture of the organization
- Risk of adding activities that may confuse employees and customers regarding the company's incentives and priorities
- Risk of defocusing the organization by trying to do everything for everybody
- Risk of shifting customers from high-value activities to low-margin ones
- Risk of legitimizing the new business, thus creating an incentive for still more companies to enter this market

---

The existence of such trade-offs and conflicts means that a company that tries to compete in both positions simultaneously risks paying a huge straddling cost and degrading the value of its existing activities (Porter, 1996). The task is obviously not impossible but it is certainly difficult. This is the logic that led Michael Porter to propose more than twenty years ago (1980) that a company could find itself "stuck in the middle" if it tried to compete with both low-cost and differentiation strategies.

Porter (1996) identified three main factors that give rise to these trade-offs. First, trade-offs arise from inconsistencies in a company's image or reputation. Firms that try to offer two different kinds of value that are not consistent with each other run the risk of jeopardizing their existing image and reputation. Second, trade-offs occur as a result of the particular set of activities that a company needs to compete successfully in its chosen position. A unique strategic position requires a particular set of tailored activities that are different from those needed in other positions in the industry. This set of activities may include different product configurations, different equipment, different employee behavior and skills, and different management systems. Many trade-offs occur because the tailored activities of a unique strategic position are incompatible with the activities of alternative positions in the industry.

Finally, trade-offs arise from the limits a firm faces when it tries to coordinate and control incompatible sets of activities. Companies that try to compete in two different strategic positions at the same time find it difficult to set the necessary organizational priorities and communicate them clearly to their employees. These companies then run the risk of losing focus through adding activities that may confuse their employees. In many cases, the latter are not clear about the overall incentives and priorities in the organization, and about what they need to do to achieve these goals. As a result, they often attempt to make day-to-day operating decisions without a clear framework and direction, which seriously undermines their performance (Porter, 1996).

The existence of trade-offs makes it extremely difficult for established firms to respond to a business-model innovation effectively. In most cases, they incur a straddling cost that far outweighs any potential benefits emerging from the new positioning. Put in a different way, a company cannot compete in both positions simultaneously without experiencing major inefficiencies. Any attempt to manage the innovation by utilizing its existing systems, processes, incentives, and mind-sets will only suffocate and kill the new business.

It is in this sense that business-model innovations are sometimes called strategic innovations (Markides, 1997). The term *strategic* is not used to mean "important" or "big." Consistent with the resource-based view of the firm, an innovation is considered strategic if it is difficult for competitors to imitate, substitute, or replicate quickly. And what makes it difficult to imitate is (among other things) the fact that the value-chain activities of the new business model are not only different from but also incompatible with an established company's existing set of activities.

Therefore, to summarize the discussion so far: business-model innovation is the discovery of a different and difficult-to-imitate business model in an existing industry that attracts new customers to the offerings of that industry and so enlarges the economic pie. It does, however, display certain characteristics that make it quite unpalatable to established firms (see box).

Who Wants to Be a Business-Model Innovator?

Given the characteristics of business-model innovations, it's not exactly clear why any self-respecting established company that already has a winning business model would want to discover another one! Sure, for new entrants and smaller companies, this is a no-brainer—the best way for smaller companies to attack big competitors is through guerrilla tactics (Porter, 1985, chapter 15). But why would any established company want to develop a new business model, especially if its existing one works fine? And why would the established firm want to get involved with a new business model that would most likely lead it to low-margin customers and create all kinds of conflicts with its existing business model?

The Characteristics of New Business Models That Make Them Unpalatable to Established Firms

- New business models emphasize different product or service attributes from those emphasized by the traditional business models of the established firms. As a result, their offerings are—at least initially—of no interest to the customers of the established firms.

- The markets created around the new business models start out as small and insignificant relative to the main markets of the established firms. As a result, it is difficult to generate entrepreneurial passion for the new markets within the established firm.

- The new markets take time to grow and take even longer to turn profitable enough for the established firms. As a result, they run into the "impatient capital" problem that all publicly traded companies face.

- The new business models create markets that have different key success factors from the ones in operation in the established firm's main market. This implies that the firm needs to put in place a different combination of tailored activities (such as value chain, structures, cultures, and internal processes) from the ones that it has in its established business.

- The new set of activities required for the new market is not only different from but often conflicts with the set of activities that the firm has in its main business. These conflicts encourage the managers of the established business not only to withdraw their support for the new business but even to sabotage and suffocate the innovation.

- New business models eventually invade the established market and cannibalize the existing business model. As a result, the managers of the organization view them more as a threat to repel than as an opportunity to exploit.

Furthermore, suppose that the established firm decides to go ahead with a new business model. The dilemma then is how can its people continue managing their existing business with one business model while at the same time serving another customer segment in the same business with a second business model. This challenge is not the same as trying to serve different customer segments with different brands, as Unilever or P&G or Volkswagen or General Motors or Mercedes do. Sure, VW sells its Audi brand to one customer segment, its VW Golf brand to another, and its SEAT brand to another—but the company still operates under the same business model no matter what customer segment it is serving. The issue with business-model innovation is not how to offer different brands to different customers but how to operate two different (and often conflicting) business models in the same business.

Not that the challenges for established firms end there. Suppose they decide that rather than operate with two business models, they'd rather migrate from their existing business model to the new one. How, then, could they manage the migration process? Or suppose that they'd rather focus on their existing business model—how then could they respond to the invading business model? Adopting the new business model is only one of the many options available to established firms—what else could they be doing and how?

I raise all these questions to make two important points. First, it should be clear that business-model innovations are not necessarily superior to the business models that established companies already employ. This means that it is not necessarily an optimal strategy for an established company to abandon its existing business model in favor of something new or to grow the new model alongside its existing business model. The decision should be based on a careful cost-benefit analysis and would depend on the specific circumstances of the firm as well as the nature of the innovation. The decision should also take on board any other growth opportunities that the established firm may have at its disposal—such as diversifying into adjacent markets or taking its existing business model internationally. Given the other growth options (and given its limited resources), the decision to invest in the new business model may rank low on a company's priority list.

Second and more important, bear in mind that the challenge that an established firm faces is not so much how to discover a new, game-changing business model as how to overcome some of the unpalatable characteristics that new business models display. What can the firm do to make these new business models less conflicting or more attractive to the existing business? Established firms can encounter endless advice on how to discover new business models, but they will take no action until they adopt organizational structures and processes that make these innovations more palatable. Therefore, my task in the chapters that follow is to propose the organizational solutions that a big firm must put in place to allow it to pursue business-model innovations.

It should be clear from the questions raised so far that I aim to examine business-model innovation primarily from the perspective of an established company. The established company already has a business to manage, operates a certain business model (or strategy), and competes within certain mind-sets, politics, and realities. These are the questions that this company's leadership might be thinking about:

- How could I discover a new business model in my business?
- How can I convince my organization (and win emotional commitment) to embark on such a journey?
- If I succeed in developing a new business model, how can I implement it in an efficient way?
- If I do succeed in implementing a new business model, how can I operate with two business models in the same industry simultaneously?
- If somebody else discovers a new model in my industry, how should I respond to it?

- When should I pursue business-model innovation in a proactive way?

This book aims to answer these questions. In the next chapter, I start the journey by answering the first question—how could a firm discover a new, game-changing business model in its industry? Specifically, how could it create the necessary organizational sense of urgency (or positive crisis) that would propel the organization out of its inertia and old mind-set?

Summary

- Business-model innovation is the discovery of a different business model in an existing industry. The innovation enlarges the market by attracting nonconsumers to the product or service or by encouraging existing consumers to consume more.

- New business models invade the market by offering a different value proposition from what the established players are offering. As a result, they attract different customers from those of the established firms. To serve these different customers, the innovators need to develop a business system that is not only different but also conflicts with the business systems used by the established players.

- These characteristics make business-model innovations unpalatable to most established firms. It is mostly new start-up firms who find this kind of innovation attractive. The established firms will actively pursue this kind of innovation only when they put in place organizational structures and processes that make the new business model less conflicting and more palatable to them.

2

DISCOVERING NEW BUSINESS MODELS

How could a company discover a game-changing business model in its industry? Several authors have provided excellent advice on how a company could systematically analyze its markets to identify new, revolutionary ways of competing. For example, Kim and Mauborgne (1999, 2005) proposed six analytical techniques that companies could use to develop "blue ocean strategies" and discover new market space in their industries:

- Look across substitute products: Home Depot (do it yourself versus hiring contractors); Intuit (Quicken Software versus pencil).
- Look across strategic groups: Polo, Ralph Lauren; Toyota, Lexus.
- Look across buyer groups: Bloomberg, focused on individual traders rather than IT managers.
- Look across complementary products: Barnes & Noble.
- Look across the functional-emotional orientation of your industry: Swatch; Starbucks.
- Look across time: Apple iPod; Cisco.

Similarly, Hamel and Prahalad (1991) emphasized the importance of corporate imagination in identifying "white spaces" in one's industry and proposed a number of mind-expanding strategies to do so:

- Escape the tyranny of the served market: Who is your customer? What is your business?

- Search for innovative product concepts.
- Overturn traditional price and performance assumptions.
- Get out in front of customers and employ expeditionary marketing.

Numerous other authors—far too many to list here—have also developed a seemingly endless list of tactics and analytical techniques to help companies discover new business models—interested readers are referred to the work of Barney (2006), Bryce and Dyer (2007), Christensen and Raynor (2003), D'Aveni (1994), Grant (2007), Hambrick and Fredrickson (2001), Hamel (1996), Hammer (2004), Kim and Mauborgne (1997 and 2005), Markides (2000), McGrath and MacMillan (2000), Porter (1980, 1985), Slywotzky (1996), and Stalk, Pecaut, and Burnett (1996).

Without wanting to belittle the importance of analysis in generating breakthrough ideas, it is important to appreciate that this is only one of many ways that a company could use to come up with new, game-changing strategies. The truth of the matter is that the process of developing a superior strategy is part planning, part gut feeling, and part trial and error until you hit upon something that works. Developing a new strategy must encompass all elements in this spectrum. It would take a hopelessly romantic planner to argue that in-depth analysis alone is what creates masterful strategies. However, it would be equally silly to pretend that analysis and thinking are not necessary ingredients and that intuition and trial and error alone will give rise to a winning strategy. Both are essential elements: analysis sketches the skeleton of a possible strategy; experimentation makes it possible to refine, add, or change that original skeleton altogether.

To highlight these points, let's consider a number of cases of successful game-changing strategies. For example, in 2005, Tim Spalding started a social network called LibraryThing, which is based not on who you know but on what books you have read. You can list your first two hundred books on the site for free but displaying more costs $10 a year or $25 for a lifetime membership. The venture turned profitable from year one, and just two years after it got started, its users had listed or recommended more than ten million books, making it the third-largest private library in the United States. It's now moving into the bookstore market and plans to get into the business of advising libraries on how to manage their catalogs. It's certainly a successful venture with a unique business model, but how did Tim Spalding come up with the idea? According to him, it all came from an experience he had when he was nine years old.[1] At that age, he used his first computer to make lists of the books he owned. To create LibraryThing, he simply created an online version of his original Apple application, allowing anyone to post their books.

How about the idea behind ING Direct, the branchless direct bank that belongs to the Dutch financial-services conglomerate ING? In the ten years since its creation, the bank has become the largest Internet bank in the United States with additional operations in Austria, Australia, Canada, France, Germany, Italy, Spain, and the United Kingdom. It targets low-maintenance and self-service-oriented customers and offers them simple and easy-to-understand financial products through the Internet, by phone, or by mail. It has attracted customers through its high-interest savings accounts and lack of service charges or minimum account balance requirements. Its low-cost, low-margin, high-volume business model attracts 150,000 new customers every month.

Apparently, the idea behind the bank's successful business model was born out of necessity—ING did not have the necessary resources to build a proper bank in the U.S. market, so it opted to try something new and cheap. Ten years ago, the Dutch financial-services conglomerate ING had its home market locked up and was looking to expand around the world. But buying or building enough branches to break into a mature market like the United States would be hugely expensive. So the company decided to run an experiment, communicating with customers only by phone, mail, and the Internet. With the money saved, ING Direct could offer a significantly higher interest rate on savings accounts, a handy way to capture customers from conventional banks. Obviously, the experiment turned out to be a good one!

How about the idea behind the introduction of the most successful toy ever—the Barbie doll? The story goes that Ruth Handler got the idea on a family vacation in Switzerland in 1957. She saw a doll there named Lilli, which was primarily used by men as a sex toy. She brought the idea back to the United States and used it as the platform to develop and introduce Barbie in 1959. And the idea behind Netflix, the online DVD rental upstart that reached the $1 billion sales mark within ten years of being created? That was born out of customer frustration with what the market was offering at the time. Reed Hastings was inspired to start Netflix in the United States when a video store charged him a $40 fine for returning his rented video late.

And finally, where did the ideas behind the successful IKEA strategy in the furniture industry come about?

> When Ingvar Kamprad, IKEA's founder, tried to crack this market, he was shut out at every turn. Barred from selling directly at trade fairs, he resorted to taking orders there. When that was forbidden, he contacted customers directly (initiating a profitable mail-order business, which necessitated that the furniture be easy to ship). When Swedish manufacturers refused his business, Kamprad sourced from Poland, getting even better prices than before. Locked out of traditional outlets, Kamprad converted a factory into a warehouse and showroom, where explanatory tags, self-service, a colorful catalog, and the lure of instant availability— thanks to on-site stocking—were deliberately distinctive. In every instance, the strategy was driven as much by necessity as it was choice. . . . In hindsight, IKEA's positioning is indeed brilliant and is indeed a source of real and sustainable differentiation. The position, however, was as much a consequence of adaptability as it was

of strategy. It was persistence—and experimentation under the strict discipline imposed by constrained resources—that allowed IKEA to build its furniture franchise.[2]

What is the moral of these stories?

These stories demonstrate that the list of tactics that a company could use to enhance its corporate creativity is potentially infinite. As if this point is not obvious enough, consider Table 2.1, which lists a number of business-model innovators

Table 2.1. How to Discover New Business Models.

Innovator	Source of Innovation
Enterprise	Saw the growth of a new customer segment (or customer need) as demographics changed.
Mattel (Barbie)	Targeted a different customer and *created* a new need in this customer (aspiration).
Canon	Targeted a different customer, focused on a new customer need, and built on existing core competences.
Swatch	Offered what the competitors were offering (good enough in price) and created a new product benefit (design and fashion).
Bright Horizons	Targeted a different customer.
Sara Lee (Senseo Coffee)	New trends in society gave rise to new customer segment.
Body Shop	Offered what competitors were offering (good enough in cosmetics) and created a new product benefit (environmentally friendly).
Charles Schwab	Offered what competitors were offering (research and advice) and created a new product benefit (cheap and easy).
Honda	Targeted a new customer segment and offered a new benefit.
Southwest	Targeted a new customer segment and offered a new benefit.
Starbucks	Redefined what the benefit (or value proposition) of the product is.

and the main source of the innovation for each. As the old saying goes: "Ideas come from anybody, anytime, anywhere."

However, there is a catch. For any of these tactics to work, the organization must first adopt the right mind-sets and attitudes. Specifically, unless the company institutionalizes a healthy questioning attitude that encourages senior management to (continuously) question its current business model, none of these tactics will work in practice. Thus, a prerequisite to business model innovation is proactive and continuous challenging and questioning of the way that a company currently operates. Specifically, the organization must focus its questioning in four areas:

- The definition of what business the firm thinks it is operating in
- The firm's current Who-What-How position, that is,

  Who its customers really are

  What it offers them

  How it plays the game

Therefore, rather than add to the list of tactics that companies could use to enhance their creativity, I'd like to use this chapter to first explore why these areas are fertile ground for producing business-model innovation and then describe how to get a *successful* organization to actually engage in proactive questioning of its current way of operating (rather than simply talking about it). For interested readers, Appendix B describes a few additional tactics that could be used to enhance corporate creativity.

Redefine the Field—What Business Am I In?

The behavior of every individual is conditioned by their individual mental model of the world. Similarly, the behavior of every organization is conditioned by its dominant mental model.

Appendix B describes mental models in more detail—what they are, how they get created, and how individuals can escape from the constraints of their mental models.

Perhaps the *most dominant mental model that any company has* is its perception of what business it is in. The definition that a company gave to its business a long time ago (either explicitly or implicitly) conditions how that company sees its business, which in turn determines how that company is going to play the game in that business (that is, its strategy or business model). This suggests that one of the most effective ways for a company to come up with a different business model is by questioning its existing definition of its business.

In fact, this is exactly what happens with successful business-model innovators. When you examine successful innovators, the first thing to notice is the obvious: they are all following tactics that are very different from the tactics of every other competitor in the industry. If you probe further, you begin to see what is behind these tactics—the thinking process that managers went through and the questions they asked to come up with these tactics. But it's necessary to take an additional step back into the minds of these managers to discover the source of the innovation. In most cases, the source of business-model innovation is an honest questioning of the answer that managers had given a long time before (either explicitly or implicitly) to the question: "What business am I in?"

Think about it. What business a company believes it is in will determine who it sees as its customers and its competitors, what it regards as its competitive advantage, and so on. It will also determine what it thinks the key success factors in its market are and thus ultimately determine how it will play the game in this market—its strategy. If a company starts competing in a totally different way from everyone else, the reason may be that it sees itself competing in a different business altogether.

Rosenbluth Travel, a family-owned travel agency that was acquired by American Express in 2002, provides a fascinating illustration of the power of business redefinition. Under the stewardship of Hal Rosenbluth, the company grew from a $20 million business in 1978 to a $15.5 billion global travel management company by 2002. Rosenbluth explained the success of his company in these words: "Our biggest advantage was to understand that as deregulation changed the rules of travel, *we were no longer in the travel business so much as we were in the information business*" [emphasis added].[3] This fundamental rethinking of the business allowed Rosenbluth to take a series of actions (such as acquiring computers and airline reservation systems, developing a private reservation data system and relational databases, and so on) that, to an outsider, may have seemed very strange. To the people on the inside, however, all these actions made perfect sense: if you think of yourself as being in the information business rather than the travel business, this is what you need to be successful—isn't it obvious? Hal Rosenbluth claimed that the company had undergone a similar transformation about a hundred years before—when his great-grandfather had an insight about the business in 1892. He realized that "he wasn't just in travel, selling tickets to people who wanted to cross the Atlantic. He was in family immigration, getting whole clans of people successfully settled in America."

Such redefinition of the business is at the heart of business-model innovation, and it is truly remarkable how many of today's business-model innovators started out on their revolutionary journey by first redefining the business they were in. Thus Howard Schultz, president of Starbucks, does not believe he is in the coffee business. Instead, he is in the business of creating a consumption experience—of which coffee is a part. Therefore, a visit to one of his stores is "romance, theatrics, community—the totality of the coffee experience."[4] It goes without saying that if you think you are in the "coffee experience" business rather than the coffee business, you will behave very differently from any competitors who think they are in the coffee business. Not better, just differently.

Another example of successful business redefinition is provided by Apple. When they started the company, Steve Jobs and Steve Wozniak did not think they were just in the "computer business." To them, "computers were supposed to be fun"—so they were also in the toy or hobby business. This mind-set led to the user-friendliness of the Macintosh and to the first machine that allowed physical interaction with the computer by means of a mouse. Yet another example is the Leclerc organization in France: its people do not see themselves as being in the supermarket business; instead, they consider themselves "modern-day crusaders" who are out "to change modern retail distribution in France." Once it is clear that this is their conception of who they are, then many of their strategic tactics (such as undertaking more than fourteen hundred legal cases against distributors in France) begin to make sense. And consider what Robert Polet, chief executive of the Gucci Group, said to explain Gucci's moves into such things as playing cards and chocolates: "We are not in the business of selling handbags. We are in the business of selling dreams."[5]

Such redefinition of the business can come only when people ask, "What business are we really in?" It does not mean that by asking the question a new or even better definition will be discovered. But even a remote possibility of discovering something new will never come up if the question is never asked. Appendix B provides a methodology on how a company could go about redefining its business in a proactive way.

Redefine Who Really Is the Customer

The second source of business-model innovation is a fundamental rethinking of the question, "Who is my customer?" Implicit in this question is the idea that *the choice of customer is a strategic decision*—it is the company that chooses its customers and not vice versa. The criterion for choosing who will be a customer and who will not should be some kind of assessment of whether a customer is good—for that company—or not. The trick, therefore, is to identify for your company which customers are good (and keep them or go after them) and which are not (and so avoid or get rid of them). But again, a good customer for one company may be a bad customer for another. Whether a customer is good or bad depends not only on the intrinsic characteristics of that customer—such as its willingness and ability to pay on time or its profitability—but also (and primarily) on whether a company is able to serve that customer better or more efficiently than its competitors as a result of its unique bundle of assets and capabilities.

This point may seem obvious, but how many companies actually think about the question in an explicit and proactive way? How many have a list of explicit criteria by which they judge every customer? More important, how many companies actually get rid of existing customers that they have identified as bad customers?

In terms of business-model innovation, the purpose of thinking strategically about this question is to either identify new customers or to re-segment the existing customer base in a more creative way and thus create brand-new customer segments. Many companies seem to believe that new customer segments emerge only when new customer needs emerge. The emergence of new customer needs is certainly an important source of new customer segments but it is not the only one. Often, customer needs remain the same but customer *priorities* change—for example, customers still need both warmth and style from their overcoats, but compared to thirty years ago, style has certainly risen (for whatever reason) on the list of customer priorities, creating an opening for someone set up to offer particularly stylish overcoats. Thus a company that identifies such changing priorities (not needs) can carve out a specific customer niche of customers who place high value on something that company can provide better than any of its competitors.

Similarly, a company may identify a specific customer segment that is currently not being served by existing competitors. The reason these customers are not served is not that companies have not identified their needs. They may know the needs but have decided that the customer segment is not big enough to go after, or that they cannot serve this segment profitably given their existing setup. If a new company can set itself up in such a way as to serve this niche efficiently, then it would have a new customer segment at its disposal—not because any new customer needs have emerged but because it has found a more efficient way to cater to existing needs. If this niche actually grows later on, then the company would have a big segment at its disposal.

A third way to identify new customer segments is by more creatively segmenting the existing customer base and so putting different kinds of customers together according to a new logic. Recombination of existing customer segments may also allow a company to create a new need and then grow a particular segment.

My goal is not to make an exhaustive list of all possible ways a company can identify new customer segments. Rather, I want to suggest that new customer segments can be developed not only as a result of new customer needs but in a variety of ways (see box). However, a company will not really identify new segments unless it proactively thinks about the question, "Who really is my customer?"

How to Discover New Customer Segments

- Look for customer segments that competitors are either ignoring or underserving. (Examples: Paychex, WellPoint Health Networks, Southwest.)
- Identify changing customer needs or priorities and develop product offerings to meet these new needs. (Examples: Barbie, Senseo Coffee.)

- Re-segment the market in a creative way so as to merge smaller customer niches. (Examples: Progressive Insurance, IKEA, Home Depot.)
- Create a new customer need and build the customer segment around it. (Examples: Swatch, Body Shop.)
- Remove functionality from overengineered products and attract customers to a simpler version. (Examples: Canon, Honda, Palm.)
- Segment the market by customer needs (rather than demographics) and focus on new or underserved needs. (Examples: Enterprise Rent-A-Car, Sephora, MinuteClinic.)
- Target a different customer from those that traditional competitors focus on. (Examples: Bright Horizons, Bloomberg, Dermalogica.)
- Exploit technology to offer a new value proposition to customers. (Examples: Amazon, Schwab, CNN.)

Inevitably, if a company identifies a new customer base, it will develop a business model to cater to the specific needs of these customers. This business model will most probably be different from the ones that established competitors use to serve *their* customers. Thus, this company will be breaking the rules in this industry not because it set about doing so but because what it does is exactly what its chosen customer segment wants.

Many of the business-model innovators listed earlier in the book started out this way—they first identified a customer segment (usually but not always at the low end of the market) or a customer niche that was not properly served by existing competitors. They then designed their products and delivery systems to fit the requirements of this customer segment. What they ended up with was a business model that was fundamentally different from the ones used by their mainstream competitors who were serving the mainstream customers. This source of business-model innovation underpins the success of companies such as Wal-Mart, Canon, Apple, Southwest Airlines, the Body Shop, Texas Instruments (in personal calculators), Lan & Spar Bank, J.C. Penney (back in the early 1900s), USA Today, Komatsu, Honda (in motorcycles and cars), and many more.

For example, consider Herb Kelleher, CEO of Southwest Airlines. At a time when other airlines were using hub-and-spoke systems, he decided to adopt a different business model. But how did he come up with the unique Southwest business model? According to him: "We wound up with a unique market niche: we are the world's only short-haul, high-frequency, low-fare, point to point carrier. . . . We wound up with a market segment that is peculiarly ours and everything about the airline has been adapted to serving that market segment in the most efficient and economical way possible."[6]

Consider also the example of Enterprise Rent-A-Car. This company is today America's biggest car rental firm. Its founder achieved this on the back of a business model that focused not on the traditional customer segment (that is, people who rent cars at airports) but on people who rent cars for whatever reason other than for travel—for example, people whose cars are in the shop for repairs or people whose cars were totaled in accidents and need new vehicles in a hurry. By targeting the replacement market, Enterprise developed a business model to cater to this market. Needless to say, this business model is different from that of Hertz and Avis, both of which target travelers. For example, whereas Hertz and Avis locate their offices at airports, Enterprise has its 2,400 offices within fifteen minutes of 70 percent of America's population and picks up customers from their homes at no extra cost.[7] Similarly, rather than use travel agents to push its service to end consumers—as Hertz and Avis do—Enterprise has focused on insurance companies and mechanics to do its push marketing.

Just choosing a customer niche that's different from the customers existing competitors focus on will not necessarily lead a company to a new and game-changing business model. For this to happen, the niche must grow significantly, either because the new business model attracts nonconsumers into the market or because existing consumers are encouraged to consume more. In other words, the new business model helps grow the total market. This will take place only if the new business model offers something (such as *new* benefits) that increases demand. Thus, identifying a new customer niche is only the start of the innovation. The company must still build a business model to cater to this new customer and attract new customers to its offering.

Overall, therefore, business-model innovators emerge in the following manner: At any given time, the mass market is served by a number of competitors. For whatever reason—through gut feeling, analysis, intuition, trial and error, or plain luck—another company spots an underserved customer segment or a newly emerging customer niche. It goes after it. The existing competitors do not bother about it because the innovator is not really taking customers away from them—they still control the mass market. Given the way the new company competes in its little niche, they may not even see it as a competitor. Over time, however, the niche grows either by stealing market share from existing competitors or by attracting nonconsumers into the market. At this point, competitors take notice and search frantically for a reply. In the meantime, academics the world over label this company a maverick competitor who won through business-model innovation and start writing glowing case studies about it!

This scenario seems to fit the success stories of companies like Canon, Apple, Southwest Airlines, Wal-Mart, Dell, Snapple, CNN, MTV, and Nucor perfectly. What eventually led to the success of these companies was the choice of a specific market niche that grew phenomenally. But what does it mean to say that "the niche grew phenomenally"? It means that what was important to only a few people is now important to many more. For example, concern for the environment grew in the 1980s and along with it the fortunes of the Body Shop. How did this happen? Either the need was already there and a company was lucky or quick enough to climb on the rising wave just in time, or the company helped grow this need by making every customer aware of it. This suggests that the important thing for business-model innovators is to pick a niche whose needs will grow in the future—that is, pick the right niche.[8]

How do business-model innovators pick the right niche? There is no magic formula. Picking the right niche requires a deep understanding of customer needs and priorities and how these are changing in the future. It also requires the courage (most vividly seen in entrepreneurs) to actually take the risk to pursue what appears to be a promising customer segment but which may very well turn out to be a fatal mistake.

Redefine What You Are Really Offering This Customer

The third source of business-model innovation is an honest rethinking of the question, "What products or services should I be selling to my customers and what is my value proposition to these customers?" Implicit in this is the notion that *the choice of products or services is a strategic decision:* companies should decide in a strategic way what to offer their customers. Many companies seem to believe that the choice of customers automatically leads them to the choice of products and services they should be offering. This may be the case, but from a business-model innovation perspective it also helps to reverse the order in this thinking. Thus instead of saying, "These are our (new) customers so let's think what they want so we can offer it to them," it may help to start the thinking like this: "These are the (new) products or services that we want to offer so let's think who would want to buy them."

Thinking strategically about what to offer the customer should be part of any strategy process. However, for business-model innovation to take place a company would have to be the first to identify new or changing customer needs or wants or priorities and therefore be the first to develop new products—or, even better, *new value propositions* for the same product.

Recall from Chapter One that what business-model innovators do is to offer the same product (or service) as their mainstream competitors but emphasize different product (or service) attributes from those emphasized by the traditional business models of the established competitors—in other words, they offer the same product (or service) but sell it on the basis of a different value proposition. Thus, whereas Xerox emphasized the technological prowess of its copiers and their superior copying speed, Canon attacked by emphasizing the (low) price and (high) quality of its copiers. And whereas Seiko and Timex sold their watches on the basis of accuracy and functionality, Swatch took the market by storm by emphasizing the style and design of its watches. Table 2.2 lists a few business-model innovators who exploited this strategy.

Table 2.2. Innovating by Offering the Same Product but Selling It on a Different Value Proposition.

Value Proposition of Established Competitors	Value Proposition of Innovators
Xerox: Speed of copying	Canon: Good enough in speed of copying and superior in price and quality
Merrill Lynch: Research and advice	Schwab: Good enough in research and advice and superior in price and speed of execution
Seiko: Accuracy, price, functionality	Swatch: Good enough in price and superior in style
Gillette: Closeness of shave	Bic: Good enough in closeness of shave and superior in price and convenience

Barnes & Noble: Experience, service, and environment	Amazon: Good enough in service and superior in price, availability, and convenience
British Airways: Number of destinations, frequency of travel, service	easyJet: Good enough in service and destinations and superior in price
Harley-Davidson: Speed and power	Honda: Good enough in speed and power and superior in size and price
US Steel: Quality	Nucor: Good enough in quality and superior in price
Traditional universities: Research-based, quality education, and career placement	University of Phoenix: Good enough in quality of education and superior in flexibility and price
Traditional banks: Personal service, branch network, and product availability	ING Direct: Good enough in service and superior in price and convenience

Not all new value propositions are necessarily good value propositions, so it is important for a company to evaluate its ideas before rushing to offer them to customers. At least three criteria must be met before deciding to offer a new value proposition. Specifically, the company needs to ask the following questions:

- Is the new value proposition substantially different from what's on offer at the moment?
- Is there a big enough customer segment that might be interested in the new value proposition?
- Is it difficult for competitors to imitate, replicate, or substitute the new value proposition?

How do innovators discover new value propositions to offer? The first and obvious way to do so is, of course, to ask the customers. However, although absolutely necessary, it is important to appreciate that simply asking the customers (or monitoring customer changes) does not necessarily lead to the breakthrough ideas on which new business models are based. There are many reasons for this.[9] By far the most important is the simple fact that customers can only tell you their needs or wants, but what actually needs to be done to satisfy these needs requires a creative leap on the part of the company. And this is extremely difficult.

Consider, for example, the case of a German company that manufactures coffee percolators.[10] When it asked customers what they wanted from their percolators, the customers said "good quality coffee." The problem the company immediately faced was that what needed to be done (to the machine) to achieve this customer need was not obvious. What can you really do to your coffee machine to offer the customer a high-quality mug of coffee? And can you do it in a cost-efficient way so as not to make the machine prohibitively expensive? It required a lot of creativity to actually come up with concrete ideas to satisfy this need. It should be obvious that identifying what the customers want is easy—just ask them! But the creativity breakthrough will come only from a jump beyond the obvious—to truly understand what is behind what the customer is saying and what products or services can be developed to satisfy the customer's needs.

Asking the customers is only one way to identify new products or services—or new value propositions. Equally important is to develop a deep understanding of a customer's business and how this customer is satisfying its own customers' needs. In this way, you can think ahead of the customer and identify new services to offer before anyone there even thinks of them. The question is, How do you get a better understanding of your customers' business? Several tactics can be used: talk to their customers, talk to their competitors, talk to their suppliers, talk to their employees, understand their value chain, become partners with customers, monitor noncustomers, monitor new entrants. . . .

To truly understand its customers, a company needs to become customer-oriented (rather than supply-oriented). This, however, is easier said than done. A company that aspires to become more customer-oriented will have to, at the very least, change its underlying culture, structure, systems, and incentives to allow its people to achieve this goal. Simply pronouncing the virtues of customer orientation without fundamentally changing the underlying organizational environment to achieve this will not deliver any results.

Benchmarking can be a useful source of new trends and new products. For example, Hanes came up with its innovative idea to distribute women's pantyhose through supermarkets when, in 1968, the president of the Hanes hosiery division, Robert Elberson, noticed that a West German pantyhose manufacturer had introduced its line (Lady Brevoni) to supermarkets in several metropolitan areas in the eastern United States. Similarly, the Kresge Co. transformed itself into K-Mart in the late 1950s, after its president Harry Cunningham had spent two years studying discount stores (and especially Korvette) all over the United States.

Another useful tactic is to continuously experiment with new products until you hit upon a new (latent and not obvious) need. For example, more than a thousand new soft drinks appear annually in Japan, with only 1 percent actually making it through the year.[11] The moral is that you will not create a new niche or discover a latent consumer need unless you try.

Again, I do not want to develop a laundry list of tactics that companies can use to discover new value propositions for their customers. The important thing is to appreciate that the bottleneck is not the availability of tactics but the mind-sets that constrain the thinking of managers. And the biggest mind-set that needs to be challenged is the belief that whatever product or value proposition made the company successful will keep it successful. It won't. The company must be constantly on the alert, searching for new product benefits and new value propositions to offer to customers. And such a search will never begin unless people ask, "What are we really offering the customer?" It does not mean that every time someone asks the question something new will appear. But companies will *never* discover anything new if their people never ask the question.

Redefine How You Play
the Game in This Industry

Asking customers or thoroughly understanding the customers' business or becoming a truly customer-oriented company can all be important drivers of business-model innovation. But is that enough? For example, did Sony really come up with the Walkman by focusing on the customer? Did Yamaha develop its electronic pianos as a result of a deeper customer understanding? Although the answer to both of these questions may be yes, this line of questioning points to another possible source of business-model innovation: building on the organization's existing core competences to create a new way of doing business that is totally different from the way existing competitors currently do business.

The first and most obvious way that a company can build on its existing competences is by transferring and applying them in another market. For example, Canon had developed a deep knowledge of the end consumer as a result of its camera operations and had an established dealer network as well. What better solution than to take these two valuable assets and employ them in the photocopier business by developing personal copiers and targeting the end consumer (rather than do what Xerox was doing, which was selling big copiers to corporate customers)? To an outsider or to Xerox, Canon's actions appear unorthodox— but for Canon, they were just a matter of building on existing strengths.

Another fascinating example of the same principle is provided by 3M. The company sells more than $2 billion worth of microreplication products every year, ranging from smart adhesives to liquid crystal display film. Apparently, all of these products stem from a single technology which was first applied in the overhead projector lens forty years ago. According to the inventor of this first microreplication product, Roger Appeldorn, nobody planned for these products: "We didn't sit down and say, 'Microreplication is the next thing to do; let's go do it.' It doesn't work this way. It evolved. It reached a critical mass. And it suddenly proliferated."[12]

Building on one's existing core competences is certainly one way to create new products or new ways of competing. However, it is not the only way—in fact, most breakthroughs happen not so much from reinterpreting existing competences as from exploiting existing competences to create and accumulate new strategic assets more quickly and cheaply than competitors can manage. This dynamic exploitation of existing core competences can come in three different ways:[13]

Use competences from one business to improve operations in another business quickly and cheaply: A company can use a core competence amassed in the course of running one business unit or division to help improve the quality of operations in another division faster and more cheaply than its competitors. For example, what Honda learns in managing its existing dealer network in the car business may help it improve the management of its largely separate network for motorbikes.

Similarly, consider the position at Canon at the time when the company had successfully established itself in both the camera and photocopier businesses. Many of the strategic assets that underpin these respective businesses cannot be shared directly—for example, the dealer networks and component manufacturing plants are largely specific to each business. But in the course of its operations producing and marketing cameras, the camera division has developed a series of competences including knowledge of how to increase the effectiveness of a dealer network, how to develop new products combining optics and electronics, and how to squeeze better productivity out of high-volume assembly lines.

This knowledge was developed in the camera business but can be transferred and used in the copier business. As a result, the copier business can get up to speed much faster and in a more cost-effective way than a competitor that has to develop this knowledge from scratch. This type of relatedness (that is, similarities in the processes required to improve the effectiveness and efficiency of separate, market-specific stocks of strategic assets in two businesses) opens up opportunities for what I call "asset improvement" advantages that allow a company to design different ways of competing in different markets.

Use competences from one business to create new assets in another business: The second way that a company can exploit its core competences in a dynamic way is by using a core competence developed through the experience of building strategic assets in one business to create a *new* strategic asset in a new business faster, or at lower cost. For example, Honda can use the experience of building motorbike distribution to build a new, parallel distribution system for lawn mowers.

Similarly, in the course of operating in the photocopier market and building the asset base required to out-compete rivals, the Canon copier division also accumulated its own, additional competences that the camera division had not developed. These may have included how to build a marketing organization targeted to business rather than personal buyers and how to develop and manufacture a reliable electrostatic printing engine. As a result, when Canon diversified into laser printers, this new division started out with an endowment of assets and arrangements to share facilities and core components. But even more important for its long-term competitiveness, the new laser printer division was able to draw on the competences built up by its sister businesses in cameras and photocopiers to create new, market-specific strategic assets faster and more efficiently than its competitors. This kind of relatedness, where the competences amassed by existing divisions can be deployed to speed up and reduce the cost of creating new market-specific strategic assets for the use of a new division, can be called the "asset creation" advantage that companies can use to break the rules.

Use competences from one business to learn new skills and grow new competences: The third way a company can dynamically exploit its core competences is by expanding its existing pool of competences, because as it builds strategic assets in a new business, it will learn new skills. For example, in the course of building a new distribution system for lawn mowers, Honda may learn new skills that allow it to improve its existing distribution system for motorbikes. Similarly, in creating the assets required to support the design, manufacture, and service of the more sophisticated electronics demanded by the laser printer business, Canon may have developed new competences that could be used to improve its photocopier business. Alternatively, combining the competences developed in its photocopier and laser printer businesses may have helped it to quickly and cheaply build the strategic assets required to succeed in a fourth market: that for plain paper fax machines.

Business-model innovation will take place when a company tries to satisfy customer needs on the basis of new sets of strategic assets, unfamiliar to existing competitors. In the process, the assets of established players become obsolete. Maverick competitors will create such new sets of strategic assets by using their core competences to either develop new assets or bundle together unique combinations of existing strategic assets. Successful innovators need therefore to identify and deploy the right core competences. A better understanding of how customers are changing leads to a better understanding of what core competences to emphasize and develop. Similarly, a better understanding of one's core competences leads to a better segmentation and choice of customers as well as a more productive development of new strategic assets that allow the company to break the rules.

Questioning Is Not Enough: Create a Positive Crisis

So far in this chapter, I have argued that it is the continuous and active questioning of what business you are in as well as your current Who-What-How choices that would lead you to new game-changing ideas. Obvious as this might seem, it's unlikely to take place, especially in successful organizations. Even when people intellectually accept the logic of questioning, they very rarely act upon it. For any action to take place, the system must be shocked out of its inertia—and this requires much more than rational acceptance of what needs to happen. This is exactly the area that differentiates successful business-model innovators from the rest.

What innovators seem to know is that it does not matter how much you encourage questioning behaviors in the organization. Eventually, the system will reach a stage of blissful stability, characterized by satisfaction with success, overconfidence or even arrogance, a strong but monolithic culture, a strong institutional memory that allows the company to operate on automatic pilot, and strong internal political coalitions. Inevitably, success will breed strong and unyielding mental models that in turn produce passive thinking. These things will happen no matter how successful you have been in institutionalizing a questioning attitude. This implies that every few years something must happen to stir things up and destabilize the system all over again.

Successful innovators excel at stirring things up. They are not afraid to destabilize a smooth-running machine—and to do so periodically, because no one can know in advance exactly when the system will need this jolt. Witness, for example, what Jack Welch did at General Electric during his twenty years at the helm. In the early 1980s, he took GE through a massive and painful restructuring program, a challenge that earned him the nickname "Neutron Jack." The restructuring was a success, transforming GE into one of the most admired corporations in the United States during the 1990s. Then, in late 1997, just when GE was posting record operating margins of 14.5 percent and a stellar 25 percent-plus annual return on equity, Welch announced a new massive restructuring program.

How can a company create shocks to the system? One powerful way, as the GE example shows, is to develop a sense of urgency in the company by purposely creating a *positive crisis*. A positive crisis is nothing more than a stretching and challenging new goal that has been sold to the rest of the organization.

The idea of creating stretch goals for the organization is not new.[14] And, as most managers know, it has lately become very popular for companies to include such goals in their mission statements. The problem is that most of these statements and stretch goals are not worth the paper they were written on.

Why might this be the case? Because a stretch goal is useless unless people buy into it—and if people are to buy into anything, an effort must be made to sell it to them. Now ask yourself: "What are the chances that a simple statement—however sexy it sounds—will, by itself, generate buy-in?" The answer is zero. No matter how grand or appealing the statement sounds, if time and effort have not been devoted to *selling* the idea to employees, it will fail to get them excited. The crucial part is selling it to every employee. A stretch goal that has not been sold to people will not create a shock to the system. To the contrary, it will lead to cynicism, negative feelings, and lack of motivation. Conversely, a stretch goal that has been successfully sold to employees will create the desired positive crisis. Done well, this will be accompanied by several physical symptoms such as passion, enthusiasm, and energy on the part of employees toward the firm and what it is trying to achieve.

Successful innovators create positive crises not by denying how well their organization was doing but by developing a new goal for the organization that makes current performance appear less than good enough. In a sense, a positive crisis is created when a CEO says: "I know we are doing quite well, but our goal now is not to just do well but to aim for the moon. Can we achieve *that?*" If the new goal is actually bought by employees, they will start questioning the way they operate. They will start saying: "We are never going to achieve that goal simply by doing whatever we are currently doing better. We need to start operating differently." Thus the stretch goal will galvanize everybody into active thinking—to question how they work, what they do, and what they have to do differently if the new goal is to be achieved. But such a wonderful outcome will emerge only if the company actually succeeds in selling the new goal to everybody and winning their emotional commitment to it.

Creating Positive Crises

How then can an organization generate the necessary commitment to its stretch goal? How can it generate enthusiasm and passion to what it is trying to achieve and so challenge people to question the status quo? The "selling process" must take employees through at least three distinct stages (see Figure 2.1):

Figure 2.1.   How to Sell a Stretch Goal.

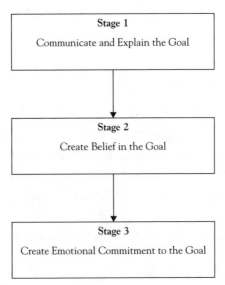

Stage 1: Communicate the goal and explain why the company has embarked on such an adventure. Communication and explanation of the organization's new stretch objective must come first. People cannot get excited about anything unless they first know what it is that they are aiming to achieve and they then understand *why* they are trying to achieve this objective. Thus time and effort must be spent to tell people the new objective so that at a certain point, everybody says: "I know what we are trying to achieve and I understand why we are trying to achieve this."

Stage 2: Create belief in the goal. The second stage is more difficult. In this stage, company leaders need to convince employees that the objective is realistic and achievable. Employees should emerge from this stage thinking: "Yes, I think we can achieve this objective." This is more difficult than it sounds. While ambitious and stretching objectives are exactly the ones that generate excitement, they are also the ones that tend to generate disbelief and dismissal as unrealistic and unachievable. To make them believable, an organization needs to go beyond words.

The most powerful tactic to convince employees that a seemingly impossible goal is indeed achievable is to generate early victories. Employees must be given proof that the ambitious goal is in fact within their reach. Thus some early victories must follow soon after the announcement of the corporate objective. The organization needs to create them, celebrate them, and use them to build momentum and enthusiasm for the objective.

Stage 3: Create emotional commitment to the goal. Finally comes the most difficult stage of the selling process, when people have to move from rational acceptance of the objective to *emotional commitment*. This is a magical jump, and at the end of it people should be saying: "Yes, I know what the objective is, I understand why we are aiming for such an objective, I believe we can achieve it, and I am personally committed to making it happen." This leap is extremely hard to achieve, and a variety of tactics need to be employed if we are to pull this off.

Among the tactics that could be used, the following are the most important:

- Make your people feel special for what they are trying to achieve and for being members of your organization. Reinforce this feeling by using symbols and rituals and by being very selective as to whom you let into the team.
- Create a credible enemy for the team.
- Create positive and negative incentives to support the chosen objective.
- Make your people feel like a team—each must think, "We are in this together; we win or lose together."
- Demonstrate through personal example the importance of the objective.
- Empower people to act on the strategy that will help achieve the objective.

The experience of Douwe Egberts—a subsidiary of Sara Lee Corp. and the market leader in ground coffee and coffee systems in Europe—in selling its new "Vision 2005" challenge to the rest of the organization highlights the difficulties and frustrations of trying to sell an organizational objective to hundreds of people. Despite being very successful, the company decided to rejuvenate itself by developing a new and challenging goal. The process was initiated in November 1995 when the top twenty managers from across the globe got together to analyze their environment and develop a new objective and a new strategy.

The new objective was communicated to the top 180 managers in a two-day conference the following April. During that conference, a variety of tactics were used to communicate the new objective and to explain why the company was embarking on such a journey. These managers were divided into groups of ten and were asked to meet periodically and discuss how the company could achieve its objective. Ideas would be forwarded straight to the CEO's office. To generate momentum, a few successful projects initiated after the November meeting were introduced at the conference (for example, the successful introduction of a new product in Spain was announced). These projects were meant to represent early victories in achieving the new objective. Finally, the conference participants were asked to consider how the new objective should be reflected in their annual operating plans and the company's incentive system. Progress toward achieving the objective, they were told, would be monitored at yearly intervals at similar conferences.

This process was repeated in every country subsidiary and every product division of the organization over a three-year period. Huge amounts of energy, resources, and time were invested in this process to make sure most people in the organization got galvanized by the new challenge facing them. Nonetheless, three years into the process, the CEO of Douwe Egberts expressed the opinion that it was only then that the rest of the organization was beginning to believe that "the new objective is here to stay!" This experience is representative of how difficult it is to get a whole organization into active thinking.

To summarize: to galvanize the organization into questioning the way it operates, its leaders must first create a positive crisis through the development of a new challenge. However, this new challenge will be nothing but empty words unless the organization takes the time (and makes the effort) to sell it to its employees and so gain their emotional commitment.

Two Caveats

It is worth reemphasizing that coming up with new ideas is one thing, actually succeeding in the market is another. I raise this point because many companies have developed game-changing business models, only to go bankrupt in the space of a few years. The case of Osborne Computer comes to mind. Very much like the founders of Apple Computer, Adam Osborne started his company in 1981 to sell a portable personal computer. In doing so, he was going after a new customer niche, which is one of the sources of business-model innovation identified earlier. In his own words: *"I saw a truck-size hole in the industry, and I plugged it."*[15] Osborne Computer grew to $100 million in sales within eighteen months—only to go bankrupt in 1983, barely another eighteen months later.

Similar stories of companies that innovated but failed abound. Readers familiar with the rise and fall of the airline People Express will no doubt see the similarities between its (failed) strategy and the (successful) strategy of Southwest Airlines. Similarly, the troubles of the new cinema concept easyCinema contrast sharply with the success of the airliner easyJet, even though both companies innovated in the same way—by offering a radically different value proposition to customers.

In addition, it is easy to cite examples of companies that tried to innovate by redefining their business (also suggested earlier in this chapter)—only to discover that this is not a guarantee for success: Xerox's attempts to go from the "copier" business to the "office of the future" business and now to the "documents" business form a case in point. The failed diversification attempts of the 1960s and 1970s on the shaky ground of a broader business definition should be a warning to all. Nor is initial success through business-model innovation a guarantee for long-term success—witness the declining fortunes of K-Mart.

All these examples of business-model innovations that failed are presented to make the point that any idea, however good, is bound to fail if it is not implemented in an effective way. Even worse, any idea, however good and however well implemented, will eventually fail if it is not supported by *continuous innovation*. While this much is true, I do not mean to belittle the importance of generating new ideas that break the rules. Just because good ideas are only one element of corporate success and are not a guarantee for success does not mean that there's no point in trying to come up with new ideas!

Finally, the point should be made that this chapter has been presented as if one individual (or a group of individuals) can sit in a room and somehow come up with all these ways to break the rules in a rational, thinking manner. This is certainly one way for innovation to take place, but needless to say it is not the only way—and it is an empirical question whether it is even the most important way. There is no question that—without throwing away the "thinking" approach—a company must also strive to institutionalize innovation. This basically means setting up the appropriate culture, structure, incentives, systems, and processes that somehow allow innovation to happen as part of day-to-day business. How 3M has institutionalized innovation could be used as a model for other companies that aspire to the same goal. A wealth of academic studies address the subject. Similarly, a company may want to identify specific obstacles or constraints that prevent it from being entrepreneurial and then somehow think of ways to remove these obstacles or bypass them. All these are important issues, but they are not the major concern of this chapter. Here, I have focused on the "thinking" approach to business-model innovation. By not talking about institutionalized innovation I do not mean to suggest that it is not an important subject. It is, but it is also a different topic that deserves a separate chapter.

Summary

- To discover new business models, firms have at their disposal an almost infinite number of ideas, bits of advice, frameworks, and analytical techniques. However, a necessary condition for creativity to take place is a fundamental questioning of a firm's existing business model and the sacred cows associated with it.

- The most important sacred cows of any firm are its definition of what business it is in, and of its existing Who-What-How position. Nothing will happen unless these things are challenged and questioned.

- Successful organizations rarely question the way they operate even when they know they should. Questioning will only take place if the leaders create a sense of urgency (or a positive crisis) in the organization.

- A positive crisis will not be created simply by giving people a stretch goal. More important than developing the stretch goal is to sell it to employees so as to win their emotional commitment to it.

3

CREATIVITY IS NOT ENOUGH: FROM DISCOVERING TO IMPLEMENTING NEW BUSINESS MODELS

Coming up with a new business model is easy! The difficult part is to implement the new strategy in an economical and effective manner, so that real value is delivered to customers in a cost-efficient way. This is what usually separates success from failure.

Webvan is a recent and prominent example. When it opened for business in June 1999 in the San Francisco Bay Area, its founder and CEO Louis H. Borders proclaimed that Webvan would fundamentally transform and simplify the way customers shop for groceries. Webvan set out to revolutionize the low-margin and intensely competitive grocery business, armed with $122 million in initial funding and a unique business model. The business model was unquestionably radical and innovative, yet Webvan turned out to be one of the Internet's most spectacular failures.

Similar stories of companies that discovered and introduced radical new business models but still failed abound. This highlights my central thesis here: dreaming up a new business model is easy. The difficulty lies in implementing it. How then could potential business-model innovators implement their radical strategies successfully?

This chapter is coauthored with Jamie Anderson of the European School of Management and Technology, Berlin, Germany. It was originally published as "Creativity Is Not Enough: ICT-Enabled Strategic Innovation," *European Journal of Innovation Management*, 2006, 9(2), 129–148. Reprinted with permission.

Obviously, many factors can influence the successful implementation of a radical new strategy—leadership, timing, resources, luck, competitor reaction, and so on. In this chapter, I focus on just one of these factors—information and communication technology (ICT)—as a key ingredient of successful implementation. ICT is not the only factor, nor is it sufficient. But I believe that for many business-model innovators, it is a key enabler to the successful implementation of their radical new strategies.

How could ICT support the implementation of new business models? To appreciate the role that ICT plays in business-model innovation, recall the last chapter's point: business-model innovation takes place when a company questions its existing Who-What-How position (or business model) in the industry and in the process discovers a new position. The starting point from which the new business model is built could be any of the following: the discovery of a new or different customer segment that requires the innovator to put in place a new business model to serve it (a new Who); the discovery of a new or different value proposition that attracts a different customer and again requires the innovator to develop a different business model to serve it (a new What); or the discovery of new or different ways of producing, delivering, or distributing existing (or new) products or services to existing (or new) customer segments (a new How).

Obviously, the first requirement to becoming a business-model innovator is to discover a new Who or a new What or a new How and then build a business model on the back of these discoveries. But being first in identifying a new position or building a new business model does not guarantee success—a company still has to exploit the new business model in a value-creating way. This is where ICT comes into play. Information and communication technology can help a company exploit a game-changing business model in four distinct ways:

- It allows a company to profitably serve customers who are new or different from those that traditional competitors target and serve. These may be customers that the established competitors are currently ignoring because it is not economical to serve them with the current business model, or they may simply be a new and emerging customer niche. ICT allows the implementation of a radical strategy that can reach these customers in a cost-effective way.

- It allows a company to offer a radically different value proposition for the same product or service and to do so in an economical way. This is possible because ICT allows the innovator to emphasize different product attributes or add new benefits to the product without adding too much to the cost base.

- It allows a company to put in place a radically reconfigured value chain that can deliver value to the customer in an innovative or economical way. Without ICT, the new value chain would have been too cumbersome or uneconomical to manage.

- It can allow a company to scale up its radical business model quickly. This protects it from competitive attacks.

I explore each of these four strategies in this chapter.

Discovering New Customers

A major source of business-model innovation is the discovery of a customer segment that other competitors are not currently serving (for example, see Rosenblum, Tomlinson, and Scott, 2003). The reason these customers are not currently served by any of the existing competitors is not that the existing competitors do not know about them or do not recognize their needs. Rather, the segment looks either too small to chase or impossible to serve profitably.

Identifying such noncustomers (Christensen and Raynor, 2003) is the first ingredient to business-model innovation. *But how could these customers be served in an economical and profitable way?* After all, the main reason the existing competitors are ignoring them is exactly the observation that they cannot be served in a profitable way. How could innovators do what the established competitors cannot do? This is where ICT comes into play—enabling innovators to implement a radical business model that is specifically designed to serve these difficult-to-serve customers in an economical way.

An Example: Edward Jones

Consider, for example, the case of Edward Jones—the brokerage that built its success in serving the needs of individual investors in rural America. Founded in 1922, Edward Jones has designed its organization to target investors who are not the high-net-worth individuals addressed by most other big brokerage firms. It aims to serve these customers by developing long-term relationships with them through its single-broker branch office network.

During the 1960s and 1970s, as major brokerage firms moved toward ever-larger offices to achieve operational efficiencies and economies of scale, Edward Jones stood fast by its commitment to deliver personalized service through the single-broker branch office network. But by the early 1980s, Jones's organizational processes were creaking under the weight of almost a thousand individual offices. As the number of offices grew, it was becoming increasingly difficult to provide brokers with the necessary training or financial and trading data and communications media at a cost that would enable the organization to remain competitive. Some within the firm believed that Jones had reached an upper limit in the number of broker offices and that further expansion would be impossible without adjustments to the Jones model. External consultants went so far as to suggest that the firm would need to move to multiple-broker offices. In fact, many in the industry predicted that the single-broker office couldn't survive.

To continue serving customers that almost nobody else wanted, Jones turned to technology. In 1985 the firm invested more than US$30 million (a substantial amount for the still relatively small firm) to move its entire broker network over to a hub-and-spoke satellite system. With a satellite dish on the branch office roof, brokers in small rural communities suddenly had access to real-time market data, video presentations by fund managers of many of the largest U.S. mutual fund management companies (to which they could invite their customers), and enhanced communications with the St. Louis headquarters and other Jones brokers. The cost of installing the satellite system did not vary by location. It was also cheaper to operate and faster and more reliable than the landline technologies used by other brokerage firms. As John Bachmann, Edward Jones's recently retired CEO, told us: "A Jones broker in Manhattan, Kansas, was suddenly able to deliver the same level of service as a broker based in Manhattan, New York."

The number of single-broker branch offices reached 3,000 by 1995, 7,500 in 2000, and exceeded 8,000 by the end of 2005. Today Edward Jones is ranked first in number of offices in the U.S. brokerage industry; it has more than 3 million retail clients and almost $2 billion in annual sales. The firm expanded into Canada in 1994 and the United Kingdom in 1997, taking advantage of its technology infrastructure to deliver the unique Jones model to both markets. The company has achieved this with an unwavering dedication to Ted Jones's original vision of serving the individual investor through a single-broker office. It will come as no surprise that the firm is currently undertaking a major project to explore next-generation broadband technologies that might enable the company to reach 10,000 branch offices globally by 2010.

Another Example: Progressive Insurance

Just like Edward Jones, Progressive Insurance has built its success on the back of ICT. While competitors were chasing the same high-margin customers, Progressive set out to target high-risk drivers—those accident-prone customers nobody else wanted. But how can an insurance company make a profit out of such clearly unprofitable customers?

Progressive's superior use of computer power for pricing and risk analysis has been recognized (Rosenblum, Tomlinson, and Scott, 2003). Less well known has been the company's development of "Claims Workbench," an ICT-enabled platform that is a key ingredient of Progressive's success in serving the high-risk segment so efficiently. This proprietary software platform is installed on the laptop of every claims representative and allows Progressive reps to perform up to twenty separate transactions while still in the field or at the scene of an accident. Rather than waiting days to assess a client's claim, Progressive dispatches a claims representative as soon as an accident is reported and the rep can complete all the necessary paperwork on the spot. This offers obvious advantages, considering that fraud represents one of the most significant challenges in serving the high-risk segment.

With the help of a wireless modem and a laptop installed in one of Progressive's immediate response vehicles (IRVs), representatives are empowered to settle many accident claims on the spot. One software application installed on laptops provides a listing of parts for nearly every car on the road, allowing for an immediate damage assessment. If additional data are required, the claims representative can connect to the Progressive extranet via wireless modem. Once the claim is processed it is sent remotely from the IRV to one of Progressive's claims centers, speeding up the overall claims process. This not only results in happier customers but also saves money. And perhaps most important, by enabling claims representatives to focus on inspecting accidents—rather than sitting behind a desk completing paperwork and responding to customer complaints about delays—Progressive also needs a smaller staff than it otherwise would. This means that the company has been able to efficiently serve those high-risk customers that nobody else wanted while simultaneously developing one of the lowest cost structures in the industry.

Offering New Value Propositions

As I pointed out in Chapter One, new business models invade established markets by emphasizing product or service attributes different from those emphasized by the traditional business models of the established competitors. This is an important ingredient behind their success, because it allows them to start their attack by attracting different customers from those that established companies focus on, and so appear nonthreatening to the established firms (Christensen, 1997). This buys them time to build their competences before making inroads into the traditional markets of the established players. Thus the ability to offer a substantially different value proposition is crucial to business model innovators. But again, coming up with different value propositions to offer the customer is the easy part. The difficulty lies in offering these new value propositions in ways that make economic sense. Innovating firms can use ICT to do exactly this—not only to radically redefine the value proposition of their product but also to deliver it in an economical way.

An Example: Cemex

For example, consider the cement business—where the purchasing decision is based mostly on price. The Mexican firm Cemex, the world's third-largest cement company, has succeeded in redefining the basis on which customers purchase cement. Rather than focus on the cost of cement itself, Cemex is offering its product on the basis of a new value proposition—*total cost to the customer,* a notion that includes the price of cement as well as all other costs that the customer has to incur from the moment of ordering cement until it is delivered to the construction site. Specifically, Cemex is using ICT to deliver just-in-time cement. In the traditional way of ordering cement, customers were required to order days in advance and were then provided with a four-hour delivery window during which the cement would be delivered to them. By contrast, Cemex has created business processes that enable same-day service and unlimited free order changes as standard operating procedures.

In 1994, Cemex launched a project called *Sincronización Dinámica de Operaciones:* the dynamic synchronization of operations (SDO). The goal of SDO was to free the company's delivery trucks from fixed-zone assignments, allowing them to roam an entire city or region. The company also equipped its trucks with transmitters and receivers connected to the global positioning system (GPS), thereby providing its computer systems at headquarters with precise, real-time data about the location, direction, and speed of every vehicle in the Cemex fleet. Today, Cemex can use its computer system to triangulate this information against order destinations and mixing plants, all the while taking traffic patterns into account, to ensure highly efficient delivery processes.

The company has introduced the kind of guarantee that competitors can only dream about: if a delivery load fails to arrive within twenty minutes of its scheduled delivery time, the buyer is refunded twenty pesos per cubic meter. That amounts to a discount of approximately 5 percent. With reliability exceeding 98 percent and with a vehicle efficiency increased by more than 30 percent, Cemex can afford to offer such generous guarantees. Even in the absence of these discounts, the total cost of ownership for building contractors has been significantly reduced given that they no longer have to pay workers to stand idle at a building site waiting for cement to arrive.[1] Today, Cemex is undoubtedly the best-performing large company in the cement industry. It has expanded its technology-enabled model to the United States, Indonesia, the Philippines, and Latin America. Its financial performance is the envy of the industry.

Another Example: Enterprise

Enterprise Rent-A-Car is another innovator that has redefined the value proposition of its product. While other rental car providers have ignored or underserved the rapidly expanding insurance replacement market, Enterprise has been able to dominate this segment not merely by offering replacement cars to the clients of insurance companies but by also providing a free, ICT-enabled car rental processing service to insurance companies.

Over the past decade, Enterprise has been quietly developing what it calls its Automated Rental Management System (ARMS). This is an Internet-based software application that enables insurance companies as well as Enterprise branches and auto repair shops to manage the entire rental cycle electronically. When a customer has an accident and calls in a claim, the insurance claims agent logs on to the Enterprise ARMS extranet and automatically places a rental reservation for the customer. This is a quick and efficient alternative to what was in the past a tedious, paper-based manual process that involved up to half a dozen phone calls to different rental office locations just to secure and process a replacement rental car. But ARMS is not limited to the rental process alone. The system is also connected to company-approved auto repair shops that are required to send regular electronic updates on the status of car repairs to customers and to the insurance company. It also tracks the collection of the repaired car and the return of the rental car, automatically generating an electronic invoice that is sent to the insurance company.

This has taken human interaction out of what was a cumbersome and time-consuming process, something that had a big impact on insurance companies. Enterprise has calculated that on average, 8.5 phone calls are eliminated from each rental transaction. That's about 85 million phone calls since 1993, equivalent to about 7 million hours of employee time, assuming an average of five minutes per call. The system also saves about half a day from a typical rental cycle, saving anything between $36 million to $107 million from the industry's rental costs annually. ARMS also provides insurers with access to online data about their transactions on the system, allowing them to better review and manage the rental process.[2] By late 2002, ARMS was used by twenty-two of the twenty-five biggest U.S. insurance companies. Enterprise has succeeded in transforming the previously labor-intensive replacement rental process and has streamlined the operations of insurers. This in turn has allowed it to offer its customers a very different value proposition from all other competitors, who simply provide replacement vehicles.

Putting in Place New Value Chains

By introducing a new business model, the innovator has to develop and put in place a different combination of tailored activities and an entirely different value chain. Information and communication technologies could play an important role in enabling a firm to achieve such architectural innovation. This is just as true for Edward Jones, which has been able to develop a unique business architecture supported by ICT to serve individual investors, as it is for Enterprise Rent-A-Car, which has been able to use the Internet to develop a new business process to serve the auto insurance industry. It is also true for a company that is recognized as a radical innovator in the mobile telecommunications market—Smart Communications, of the Philippines.

An Example: Smart Communications

In the late 1990s, Smart's low-cost, high-coverage marketing strategy, targeting the middle- and lower-middle-income segments in the Philippines, had delivered great success to the company. Innovations such as PureTxt 100 (a text-only prepaid card) allowed the company to deliver relatively low-cost propositions to a broad customer base. By 2002, Smart held 45 percent of the mobile phone market while its main competitor, Globe Telecom (Globe), controlled 40 percent. Sun Cellular was a distant third. Between 1998 and 2003 Smart had been recognized five times as one of the "Top 10 Philippine Companies in Terms of Corporate Leadership" by the *Far Eastern Economic Review*. But despite the company's success, industry analysts believed that the Philippines mobile telephony market was heading rapidly toward saturation. They pointed to the fact that close to 50 percent of the population in the Philippines lived below the poverty line, and that more than 65 percent of the population lived in rural areas where usage of mobile services was limited or nonexistent, even where network coverage was present. A report by research consultancy Barkawi & Partners suggested that industry saturation would peak at approximately 25 percent by 2007. Quite simply, the remainder of the population would be unable to afford mobile telephony given existing operator cost structures.

To develop a proposition to reach the low end of the market, Smart recognized that it could not benchmark others in the mobile industry—mobile network operators had not successfully developed propositions for very low-income consumers. Instead, the company looked to companies that already addressed this segment with other products and services, such as Unilever and P&G. It also undertook its own market research on consumer buying behavior. The company soon recognized that low-income customers received low weekly (and in many cases daily) wages, meaning that cash flow management was a key issue. While P100 (the lowest price for a prepaid card in 2002) was not a lot of money for a consumer from the middle class, the amount represented a significant cash outlay for a family living in poverty.

Not surprisingly, when Smart looked to Procter & Gamble and Unilever, which served this segment with fast-moving consumer goods, its people discovered that these firms had developed low-priced micro-packs (called *sachets*) for daily necessities such as shampoo, soaps, cigarettes, and food. While these sachets did not represent the most economical way of purchasing goods, they met the needs of consumers in terms of low purchase price. The vast majority of these items were sold through the country's small Sari-Sari stores (*Sari-Sari* means "varied" in Tagalog), which survived on high-turnover, low-value transactions. Indeed, *tingi-tingi* or "purchasing goods in small amounts" was part of daily life, and customer surveys revealed that poor Filipinos made an average of four trips per week to their local Sari-Sari store.

Sari-Sari owners were typically small merchants with close connections to their patrons. These merchants often provided credit when their customers were unable to afford cash purchases. It was estimated that more than 750,000 such stores were operating in the Philippines. By contrast, Smart had fewer than 50,000 resellers of its prepaid cards in 2002. But Smart recognized that to serve Sari-Sari stores in isolated rural areas with prepaid cards would be a costly and difficult operation in supply chain management. Warehousing, transportation, and pilferage costs all contributed to the minimum value at which a prepaid card could be sold profitably, and most industry experts saw this as an insurmountable barrier to serving geographically isolated low-income consumers. Smart understood that to serve this segment profitably, it would need to find an alternative to the physical distribution of prepaid cards.

In May 2003, Smart introduced a revolutionary over-the-air (OTA) prepaid reloading service offering airtime in sachet-like packages. The service, dubbed Smart Load, offered prices that were broken down into smaller denominations: P30 (US$0.54), P60 (US$1.07), P115 (US$2.06), and P200 (US$3.58). The lower the value of the load, the shorter the expiration period of the credit (see Table 3.1). Smart Load was advertised by Smart as "telecoms in sachets," and the smaller denominations targeted low-income Filipinos who purchased consumer goods in small quantities. The launch of Smart Load was accompanied by a US$4 million national marketing campaign.

With the launch of Smart Load, Smart minimized physical product distribution costs by creating a demand-response stocking system for prepaid airtime. Product distribution became faster, more efficient, and more secure. The user-friendly SMS distribution interface could be sold in a personal fashion complementary to Sari-Sari business practices. The special retailer SIMs (small electronic network access cards inside the retailers' mobile handsets) allowed retailers to open or close their retail handsets via SMS and enabled them to sell their service outside a physical location, and outside regular store hours.

To electronically reload, a subscriber (called a Smart Buddy) simply got in touch with a Smart Load retailer, chose from the

Table 3.1.   The Smart Load Service Offering.

Load	Price	Content	Load Expiry (days)	SIM Validity (days)
Economy	P30	30 text messages; 3 minutes voice calls	3	30
Regular	P60	60 text messages; 6 minutes voice calls	6	30
Extra	P115	115 text messages; 13 minutes voice calls	12	60
New	P200	200 text messages; 25 minutes voice calls	30	120

Notes: P30 = US$0.54, P60 = US$1.07, P115 = US$2.06, P200 = US$3.58.
Source: www.smart.com.

selection of Smart Load denominations, and paid the retailer. The retailer then loaded the customer's airtime to the subscriber's phone—all electronically. The subscriber received a text message indicating the new load amount once the transaction was completed. The entire transaction took place electronically.

The ability to reload electronically meant that consumers could purchase airtime even in remote rural locations. Retailers did not have to obtain stock and sell prepaid cards. The Smart Load service eventually replaced the PureTxt 100 service, and by the end of the second quarter of 2003, Smart had eliminated production and distribution of physical PureTxt P100 reload cards.

Smart's electronic distribution network created a new class of entrepreneurs, who found the business quite attractive. Smart estimated that, of the more than 500,000 retailers, approximately 90 percent were microbusinesses (neighborhood stores including Sari-Saris, housewives, and students acting as roving agents). Smart made distribution simple for these small entrepreneurs. Retailers executed transactions using a menu embedded in the special retailer SIM card by sending specially formatted text messages that executed the sale. Many Sari-Sari merchants extended their on-credit purchasing model from staples and sachets to Smart Load.

The start-up costs associated with becoming a Smart retailer were minimal. A prospective merchant needed a bank account, a GSM handset, a retailer SIM card costing P100 (US$1.79), and an initial load balance of P300 (US$5.37). Low capital requirements enabled the company to build an extensive dealer network and recruit several hundred thousand retailers in a few months. These retailers, in turn, served a broader market area since sales could take place over the phone, eliminating the need for consumers to physically travel to a retailer site. Retailers received 15 percent commission, with the most popular packages being P30 (US$0.54), P60 (US$1.07), and P115 (US$2.06). According to Smart, some retailers earned up to P1000 (US$18.00) per day in reload sales, and many retailers indicated that they could make as much selling OTA minutes as they could from other consumer goods sales, or more.

To make sales and reloads even more accessible for cash-poor customers, Smart launched Pasa ("transfer") Load in December 2003. The new system allowed consumers to transfer loads as low as P10 (US$0.18) from one account to another. By January 2004, denominations of P2 (US$0.03), P5 (US$0.08), and P15 (US$0.27) were added to the Pasa Load lineup. Pasa Load allowed airtime transfer by just keying in the mobile phone identification number of the recipient and the amount and sending it to access number 808.

The innovativeness of Smart Load in delivering mobile telephony to consumers living in poverty was recognized around the world. In 2004 the company won the Frost and Sullivan Asia Pacific Technology Award for "Most Innovative Application of the Year" and "The Best Mobile Application or Service for the Consumer Market" at the GSM Association Congress.

But Smart Load did not merely earn accolades—it also dramatically increased the analysts' estimates of the serviceable mobile market in the Philippines. Globe launched a similar service, Globe Autoload Max, in late 2003, and by September 2004, roughly 30 percent of Filipinos were active cell phone users. The figure was expected to reach 40 percent by 2005, and analysts now predicted penetration rates of 60 percent or more by 2008. By September 2003, two-thirds of Smart's prepaid users were reloading their phones electronically. As of June 30, 2004, approximately 91 percent of Smart Buddy subscribers were using Smart Load as their reloading mechanism. Smart Load, an ICT-enabled innovation, accounted for approximately 61 percent of sales derived from reloads.

Another Example: Inditex Group

Spain's Inditex Group SA, one of the fastest-growing fashion houses in the world, has also used vertical integration enabled by ICT to radically reduce the design-to-sale cycle in the apparel industry. The company has reduced traditional design-to-sale times to less than thirty days on most product lines. Fashion designers from Inditex attend premier fashion events where they use digital imaging to send pictures to the organization's concept development centers in Spain. These concepts are compared with an electronically cataloged CAD portfolio of in-house designs developed by the company's two hundred in-house designers. Within weeks new designs are manufactured in factories mainly across Southern and Eastern Europe, but also in Latin America, before being sent to test stores in key markets. Point-of-sales software is used to identify hit products, and production of these designs is then ramped up in single runs of 100,000 to 350,000 units that are distributed just in time to hundreds of other stores.

This vertically and virtually integrated model enables Inditex's core division, Zara, to replace 70 percent of the fashion items on its shelves every two to three weeks. Lacking Inditex's high level of ICT-enabled integration, competitors offer only four or five fashion ranges in a given year (typically Spring, Summer, Autumn, and Winter collections). Without the same level of supplier integration, the design-to-sale cycle for the industry is typically between three and six months. This forces Inditex's competitors to attempt to forecast fashion trends rather than act quickly to introduce products in response to actual demand. Vertical integration is the key to Inditex's innovation in the apparel industry, but it is information and communication technology that has enabled Inditex to deliver the benefits of this integration at the speed of the Internet.[3]

Protecting the Business Model
by Scaling It Up Quickly

Scaling up a radical business model allows the innovator to grow. But it also serves another useful purpose: it protects it from competitive counterattacks. ICT can help an innovator to rapidly scale up a new business model and so ensure its sustainability.

Revisiting a Few Examples

Consider again Edward Jones, the world's largest brokerage firm by number of offices. In 1978, Jones was a firm with a differentiated strategy that targeted the so-called unattractive individual investor segment. It had only 280 brokers, concentrated in Missouri and surrounding U.S. states. Within twenty-five years, Jones has grown by more than 750 percent and now operates more than 8,000 offices. It has also expanded into Canada and the United Kingdom. As noted, the firm now has more than 3 million retail clients and almost $2 billion in annual sales. This rapid scaling-up has created an intimidating incumbent for any challenger who is planning to attack the Jones position. ICT was a key enabler of this growth.

Consider also ARMS Web, Enterprise-Rent-A-Car's proprietary online system for automating the insurance replacement vehicle process. In just a decade, Enterprise has been able to dominate the insurance replacement market. This computerized system has enabled Enterprise to achieve rapid growth in an emerging niche market without overburdening the company's physical infrastructure. New users of the system can be added at incremental cost, with only minor adjustments to the Internet-based interface required for adoption of ARMS by insurers and auto repairers.

Since its inception in 1993, ARMS has been used to process more than 10 million rentals for more than 250 insurance companies. Enterprise's insurance rental segment was able to grow almost 50 percent between 1998 and 2002 alone. The company processed more than $1 billion worth of transactions through the system last year (about one-fifth of total revenues), and ARMS is now used by almost all the biggest U.S. insurance companies. Enterprise has built such a huge lead in this segment at such a fast pace that competitors will be playing catch-up for years.

Inditex has also been able to rapidly scale up its business model by using ICT. In 1988, Inditex had a dozen or so Zara stores in Spain and just one international outlet in Portugal. In 2002 alone, the Group opened 274 new retail outlets, reaching a total of 1,558 stores in forty-four countries. All of these stores are connected electronically to Inditex Group's design, manufacturing, and distribution processes, and competitors can only dream of matching the design-to-sale cycle times enabled by this level of integration. Inditex launched a home ware concept in late 2003 and is set to emerge as a competitor to established homeware companies such as IKEA.

The Case of Cisco

Another company that exemplifies the importance of scaling up a business model quickly and efficiently is Cisco Systems. Cisco was founded in 1984 by two Stanford professors, Sandy Lerner and Len Bosack, who came up with an idea for the router. A *router* is a device that allows the electronic transmission of data across networks and the Internet. As customer needs changed during the 1990s, Cisco also evolved into an end-to-end network solutions provider. Through organic growth and acquisitions, the company grew rapidly in the 1990s, quadrupling in size from fiscal 1994 to fiscal 1997 with as many as a thousand employees signing on each quarter.

As the Internet exploded, so did Cisco. By the end of 2000, Cisco had more than 35,000 employees globally—and more than $16 billion in revenues. The company grew to provide the entire foundation infrastructure for the Internet, with more than 80 percent of routers on the Internet marked with the Cisco label. Cisco provided not just the functionality required for data, but full multimedia support to handle voice, data, or video over Internet protocol (IP) networks. With the contraction of the

Internet and telecommunications sectors since 2002, Cisco has shrunk in terms of both number of employees and revenues. But the company's explosive growth from the early 1990s, and the way this growth was supported by technology, is still indicative of the power of networked IT.

Cisco recognized early that its internal systems could not scale up quickly enough to keep up with the pace of growth. A good example was sales-force training. In 1997, about 95 percent of training was done in the classroom. A training group of just fifty was responsible for training four thousand internal Cisco salespeople, as well as the company's then fifteen thousand partner organizations and thousands of customers. Newly hired sales personnel would travel to corporate or regional training sites for several five-day courses each year, with training delivered for one product line to the entire field in a classroom setting. This required up to two hundred training sessions for each course to reach Cisco's worldwide audience. This approach represented a model for extended failure, since salespeople simply could not spend the necessary time in the classroom to keep pace with frequent product introductions.

Cisco recognized that its future profitability and success would depend on a solution that could scale up to meet the needs of its growing business. But how could the company continue to grow without pushing its training and development systems past the crisis point? Should it attempt to outsource training services? Hire more training staff?

In 1997, Cisco identified e-learning as a way to provide employee training without the expense or time constraints of travel. After almost two years of development, the Field E-Learning Connection (FEC) was launched in 1999. This was a single online point-of-entry for the company's global sales force and support staff to plan, track, develop, and measure their skills and knowledge. The intranet system had links to more than four hundred learning resources, online and leader-led training courses, assessment exams, and learning road maps for the company's account managers and systems engineers. Accessibility was anytime, anywhere with full accountability through online testing and certification.

To complement FEC, Cisco also created learning portals for other key areas of its business, including manufacturing, worldwide customer service, and company audit. The company's Leadership Express is a portal of self-directed learning for Cisco managers, providing online management tools and articles on leadership, searchable by topic. Cisco also introduced video intranet training via its global broadband IP/TV network in 1999. Cisco can conduct a single update training session that reaches up to four thousand people at once, worldwide. This presentation is then archived for employees who missed the live broadcast event. The same IP/TV system has been used to broadcast presentations by Cisco executives since late 1997.

Cisco believes that its Field E-Learning Connection achieves cost savings of 40 percent to 60 percent or more versus instructor-led training, and estimates that 80 percent of sales and engineering training was conducted online at the end of 2001. But the main benefit identified by the company is the reduction in travel and in-classroom time for its employees, allowing them to spend more time with customers.

E-learning is just one example of how Cisco has used technology to scale up its business model. The company has also implemented initiatives for automated online expense claims, procurement, technical information, and employee benefits. For example, a New Hire Dashboard (NHD) portal has been developed to advise on everything from setting up an e-mail account to establishing a company pension plan. The portal has allowed Cisco to reduce the duration of its induction training by 50 percent, and the company believes that NHD saves new hires approximately fifteen minutes per day during their first three months with the company.

Another technology initiative, the Cisco status agent, provides the company's sales force as well as customers and sales partners with immediate access to critical information about the status of customers' orders. Specifically, it is used to monitor expected shipment dates, generate complete backlog reports of all Cisco orders, view line-item details for each product on order, and track shipment status with direct online links to the Federal Express and UPS tracking systems. Cisco believes that this system not only gives its sales force more timely information and greater control of orders, it also prevents billing and shipment problems before they arise. The self-service nature of the system has decreased order-related customer calls to Cisco's sales staff by more than 60 percent.

Cisco's main motivation for embarking on the various technology initiatives described here was to help the company deal with the dual challenges of explosive growth and rapid employee acquisition, as well as the desire to improve customer service by freeing employee time from administrative duties and face-to-face training. Cost reduction was also a goal. By the end of 2000, the company estimated that it was saving more than $86 million annually through the implementation of its various employee intranet initiatives.

Cisco continues to develop interactive Internet applications for all its functional departments, such as human resources, manufacturing, and finance. Despite the impact of the recent economic downturn on the organization, Cisco remains a strong case study of the role of information technology in supporting rapid growth through virtual rather than physical infrastructure.

Common Behaviors Toward Technology

In *Good to Great* (2001), James Collins argues that technology-induced change is nothing new. What was unique about the good-to-great organizations was not that they used technology to achieve their goals but that they thought about and used technology differently from mediocre firms. Specifically, technology for them was an accelerator of momentum, not a creator of it. In a similar vein, what I am proposing here is that using technology to implement radical new strategies is nothing new. What is unique about the innovators who did so successfully was the behaviors that they displayed toward technology. Specifically:

Successful innovators focused on technology as a driver of value, not just as a tool for operational efficiency.

Rather than using ICT primarily to shave cost from existing business processes, successful innovators use technology either to target new or existing customer segments that could not be served efficiently using established business processes or to offer new value propositions to their existing customer base. The focus was on value creation rather than just operational efficiency. This is true for companies as diverse as Dell Computer, Enterprise, Cemex, Cisco, Edward Jones, and easyJet.

This may sound obvious, but it's rarely applied in most companies. For example, in a recent survey of U.K.-based senior executives, the vast majority indicated that spending on ICT was focused on cost reduction and improving existing business processes.[4] Fewer than 5 percent of responders identified ICT as an enabler of innovation, and the majority viewed it as an expense rather than an investment. By contrast, business-model innovators looked at ICT as something that could not only support their strategy but also redefine it. Taking a longer-term, strategic perspective, they used ICT as an enabler of top-line growth and as a tool to reach new customers or offer new benefits to existing customers in new ways. Edward Jones's investment in satellite technology was not about shaving costs from the existing business—it was about a transformational scaling-up of the Jones business model. Similarly, Cemex's investment in ICT was about delivering a radical new value proposition for customers.

Michael Dell has often argued in favor of using ICT as a strategic rather than an operational tool. In a recent speech, he proposed that "ICT must be viewed not in terms of cost to be carefully managed but as a powerful enabler to deliver velocity, efficiency, and customer experience."[5] As argued in this chapter, ICT can also be viewed as a tool to pursue and exploit radical new Who-What-How positions in an industry that all the other competitors find unappealing.

Successful innovators are early adopters of ICT in their industry, even if the technology is already dispersed in other industries.

Another key characteristic of successful innovators is their willingness to experiment early in the implementation of emerging information and communication technologies. They may not be the first adopters of this technology anywhere, but they are frequently the first to adapt it to the unique needs of customers within their markets. This was certainly the case with regard to Edward Jones's adoption of satellite-enabled communications in the brokerage industry, and it is also true of companies such as Dell Computer, Cisco, and Cemex.

In the case of Cemex, the company actively benchmarked technology use by organizations outside the cement industry. It looked at companies confronting similar business challenges—such as delivering a product or service on a just-in-time basis. This led executives from the company to visit the FedEx hub in Memphis as well as a 911 dispatch center in Houston, where they observed different uses of ICT in very different industry contexts. Despite the fact that technologies such as GPS navigation and cellular communication were not yet widely used within the cement industry, Cemex saw an opportunity to adapt them to its own business requirements. Similarly, Internet-enabled virtual integration was used by Dell in the PC industry for many years before companies such as Enterprise and Progressive saw the opportunity to apply Internet-enabled and virtually integrated approaches to their own industries.

Successful innovators do not wait for complete technology solutions to fit their customer requirements—if necessary, they develop technologies themselves.

Successful innovators are not only early adopters of information and communication technology—in many cases they develop this technology themselves rather than wait for a complete off-the-shelf solution to address their requirements. This is true of both Edward

Jones and Progressive Insurance, but it is also true of other innovators such as Enterprise Rent-A-Car.

When Enterprise identified the need to develop a virtually integrated process for linking its own reservations management system to insurance companies as well as end users and auto repair outlets, it quickly realized that it was simply not possible to buy an off-the-shelf solution. With a development investment of $28 million in hardware, software, and staff time and $7.5 million in annual maintenance, Enterprise developed ARMS internally. Could Enterprise's competitors simply go out and buy ARMS off the shelf from a software vendor, just as they can purchase a CRM package, e-procurement solution, or financial management package? The answer is no. ARMS is a proprietary system developed by Enterprise's IS department; if competitors want to develop their own system, they will need to do so from scratch.[6]

Similarly, even though Progressive's Claims Workbench uses readily available ICT hardware, much of the *middleware* (software that enables existing hardware and software to function seamlessly) has been developed by Progressive. Dell, Cemex, and Zara have also developed middleware to integrate the ICT technologies that enable their own virtually integrated operations.

Successful innovators have CEOs who act as technology evangelists.

The implementation of ICT-enabled business-model innovation typically cuts across business processes and functions. Projects of this nature are notoriously difficult to implement successfully without explicit and visible senior management commitment. Perhaps not surprisingly, innovators benefited from technology evangelists pushing for the adoption of ICT from positions at the top of their organizations. These business leaders were not necessarily technology experts, nor did they fully understand the technical capabilities of ICT. But they did fully appreciate the importance of using ICT in a strategic way and encouraged their organizations to tirelessly pursue ICT as an enabler of innovation.

At Cemex, CEO Laurence Zambrano initiated the benchmarking study that culminated in the launch of SDO. He has also been the main sponsor of a range of other ICT investments. At Edward Jones, then-CEO John Bachmann was an early champion of new technologies in the firm. He summarized his philosophy to us as follows:

> You have to understand that Edward Jones is not about technology. We have organized ourselves around a specific social and economic need of a specific universe of consumers—namely the serious long-term investor. . . . The key has been recognizing who is the customer, what is the value to the customer, and organizing ourselves to be responsive to what we believe is this fundamental need. We recognized that to deliver on this need to cities and to small rural communities alike we would have to push the envelope in terms of the underlying technology infrastructure. This is how I encouraged the use of IT within Edward Jones—to deliver the kind of personalized service upon which the Jones model has been built. Sometimes, as was the case back in 1985 when we launched the satellite system, this has involved committing the organization to transformational change.

At Cisco, CEO John Chambers is a self-confessed obsessive in advocating the transformation of long-standing industry structures through the adoption of ICT. But again, Chambers understands that technology is simply an enabler of sound business practice that delivers customer value profitably.

Summary

- Discovery of a new business model is easy. The difficult part is to implement the new strategy in an economical and effective way.
- Many factors influence the successful implementation of a new business model. One of them is information and communication technology (ICT).

- ICT can help business-model innovators in four ways: to reach otherwise uneconomical customers in a cost-efficient way, to redefine what the value proposition (or benefits) of the offering is, to put in place a radical new value chain, and to scale up the new business model quickly.

- The use of technology to implement radical new business models is not unique. What is unique is the behaviors that innovators display toward technology. They use ICT as a driver of value, not just as a tool for operational efficiency.

4

USING DUAL BUSINESS MODELS TO COMPETE: IS A SEPARATE UNIT NECESSARY?

When the new, game-changing business model is discovered by a *start-up firm*, the only major challenge for the innovator is how to implement it successfully—a topic examined in Chapter Three. However, if the new business model is discovered by an *established* firm, another challenge emerges for the innovator—how to manage the new business model next to its existing business model. Given the characteristics of business-model innovations presented in Chapter One, it should come as no surprise to hear that conflicts and trade-offs between the two business models make their peaceful coexistence difficult. In fact, the evidence shows that most established companies that attempt to employ dual business models fail to do so successfully—exactly because the presence of conflicts means that by trying to pursue business model B, a company harms its business model A.

For example, a tour operating company that continues to sell holiday packages through travel agents while at the same time attempting to sell the same packages directly to end consumers through the Internet risks alienating its traditional distributors. Similarly, a consumer goods company that attempts to move into private label brands while still pushing its branded products risks damaging its existing brands and diluting the organization's culture for innovation and differentiation. The existence of such trade-offs and conflicts means that a company that tries to compete in both positions simultaneously risks paying a huge straddling cost and degrading the value of its existing activities (Porter, 1996). In most cases, this cost far outweighs any potential benefits emerging from exploiting the markets created by the new business model.

Given the potential to harm the main business, should an established company really be in the business of using dual business models to compete in the same industry? And if so, how could it do so successfully?

The decision whether to use dual business models or not has been the subject of intense debate in academia. According to Porter (1996), attempting to do so is a bad idea. This is because firms can build a competitive advantage in their industry only by intentionally choosing to focus in one strategic position and perform a different set of activities from those of their rivals. After all, this is what strategy is all about: choosing a unique position and supporting it with tailored activities that allow the firm to offer its customers a unique mix of value.

Porter also maintains that trade-offs are essential to strategy because they require firms to make a choice on what to do and, more important, what *not* to do as they deliver a unique mix of value to their customers. These trade-offs are vital for creating a unique and valuable strategic position involving a different set of activities from those of rival firms. They are also necessary to protect the company from potential imitators, thus enabling it to achieve a sustainable competitive advantage.

As Porter puts it: "Positioning trade-offs are pervasive in competition and essential to strategy. They create the need for choice and purposefully limit what a company offers. They deter straddling or repositioning, because competitors that engage in those approaches undermine their strategies and degrade the value of their existing activities" (1996, p. 69).

All this suggests to him that broadening one's strategy to embrace a new business model will lead to disaster. To Porter, a new business model requires a new combination of tailored activities specifically designed for competing effectively in the newly created market. These new activities will be incompatible with the company's existing set of activities as a result of all the trade-offs that exist between the two alternative strategic positions.

What to Do About Conflicts

The primary solution offered on how to solve this problem is to keep the two business models (and their underlying value chains) physically separate in two distinct organizations. This is the "innovator's solution"; it is primarily associated with Clayton Christensen's work on disruptive innovation, but other academics have advocated it as well.[1] Even Michael Porter has come out in favor of this strategy. Despite arguing that most companies that attempt to pursue dual strategies will likely fail, he has also proposed that "companies seeking growth through broadening within their industry can best contain the risks to strategy by creating stand-alone units, each with its own brand name and tailored activities" (1996, p. 77).

The rationale for this solution is quite straightforward. The presence of conflicts means that the existing organization and its managers will often find that the new business model is growing at their expense. They will therefore have incentives to constrain it or even kill it. Therefore, by keeping the two business models separate, a company can prevent its existing processes and culture from suffocating the new business model. The new unit can develop its own culture, processes, and strategy without interference from the parent. It can also manage its business as it sees fit without being suffocated by managers of the established company who see cannibalization threats and channel conflicts at every turn.

Bower and Christensen (1995) were the first to suggest this solution for business-model innovations, using the case of disruptive technological innovation as the basis for the recommendation. They proposed that an incumbent firm ought to place responsibility for building a disruptive technology business in an independent organization by forming teams into skunk-works projects to keep them away from the mainstream business. It is only through separation that the firm can avoid any potential spillover of the established corporate culture, policies, and systems that may impede the development of the new technology. Specifically: "To commercialize and develop the new technologies, managers must protect them from the processes and incentives that are geared to serving established customers. And the only way to protect them is to create organizations that are completely independent from the mainstream business" (pp. 44–45).

Companies should keep the new unit independent from their mainstream business even when the emerging market that develops around the innovation becomes large and commercially viable. Integrating the new unit into the mainstream organization can be disastrous, as major conflicts often arise between the new business and the existing one over resource allocation policies, and whether or when to cannibalize established products and services.

Cooper and Smith (1992) have also provided evidence that supports the separation solution. In a study on how established leading firms responded to various threatening technological innovations, the authors asserted that a decision to embrace the newly created business must take into consideration, among other things, the degree of organizational separation between the new and traditional product activities. Specifically, they considered whether the leading incumbents created a separate, independent organization to compete in the new technology or forged, instead, close organizational linkages between new and traditional product activities. They found that "in a number of cases where the new and traditional technologies were fundamentally different, decisions to use the established organization proved to be ill-advised" (p. 64).

Other management scholars have also addressed the potential advantages of creating a separate unit to compete in the new business. For example, Utterback (1994) argued that established firms can gain a foothold in markets generated by a radical technological innovation by setting up autonomous, independent units to exploit the organizational flexibility and entrepreneurial spirit that are required to succeed in the new environment. Utterback offered various examples of how established competitors organized separate units (or divisions) to bridge technological discontinuities.

For example, IBM successfully entered the personal computer market through a separate dedicated unit, set up far from the company's headquarters. Similarly, both Ford Motor Company and General Motors formed separate units (Team Taurus and Saturn Motor Company, respectively) to introduce new model cars in the market. In each case, Utterback (1994) argues that "the task of creating the competencies needed to successfully bridge into chosen markets hinged on creating organizations with clear mandates and a great deal of independence from the staffs, committees, and other encumbrances of their parent companies" (p. 229).

Finally, Tushman and O'Reilly (1996) suggested that another way to adopt a second business model is by creating an "ambidextrous" organization. Even though many things make up an ambidextrous organization (such as the existence of multiple, contradictory structures, processes, and cultures within the same organizational infrastructure), a major characteristic of such a solution is the requirement to keep the two business models in separate units, albeit with a few integrative mechanisms in place. Thus even this solution considers the need to separate the two business models as a prerequisite to peaceful coexistence.

Is Separation Always the Solution?

Sensible as this argument might be, the separation solution is not without problems and risks of its own. Nor does it fit very well with the evidence—companies have failed despite creating separate units; other companies have succeeded despite housing the new business model in the same organizational infrastructure as the existing one. For example, Continental Airlines and

KLM created separate subsidiaries to compete in the low-cost, point-to-point segment of the airline business but failed to make any inroads anyway. On the other side, Lan & Spar Bank in Denmark succeeded with dual business models despite keeping the second business model inside the existing organization.

Such evidence is a clear warning that creating a separate unit has both benefits and costs. Keeping a new business model separate from the existing one might help manage conflicts between the two. But the cost of keeping them separate is failure to exploit synergies between them. For example, a recent study by a group of McKinsey consultants found that "the simple injunction to cordon off new businesses is too narrow. Although ventures do need space to develop, strict separation can prevent them from obtaining invaluable resources and rob their parents of the vitality they can generate."[2] Similarly, a team of MIT researchers reported that "spinoffs often enable faster action early on but they later have difficulty achieving true staying power in the market. Even worse, by launching a spinoff, a company often creates conditions that make future integration very difficult."[3]

As these two perspectives demonstrate, there is no one right answer to the problem. If the firm kept the two business models separate, it gave the new model a fighting chance to survive without interference from the parent company but it also denied it valuable assets, resources, and knowledge that reside in the parent company. On the other hand, if the two business models were integrated, the new model benefited from the resources and knowledge of the parent but also risked inappropriate interference and mismanagement from the parent.

Four Strategies for Managing Dual Business Models

This suggests that rather than adopting an either/or perspective, companies may be better off approaching the issue from a contingency perspective.[4] Specifically, the literature suggests that two key variables influence how a firm should manage two business models simultaneously:

- How serious the conflicts between the two businesses are—because this determines whether a separation strategy would be especially beneficial or not
- How strategically similar the new market is perceived to be to the existing business—because this determines how important the exploitation of synergies between the two will be

If you plot these two dimensions in a matrix (Figure 4.1), you end up with four possible strategies to manage two different business models.[5]

Separation is the preferred strategy when the new market is not only strategically different from the existing business but also has serious trade-offs and conflicts with the established market. On the other hand, no separation is necessary when the new market is very similar to the existing business and presents few conflicts that need managing. In such a case, embracing the

Figure 4.1.   Different Strategies for Managing Dual Business Models.

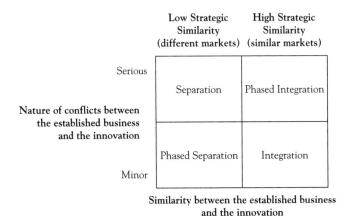

Similarity between the established business
and the innovation

new business model through the firm's existing organizational infrastructure is the superior strategy.

An interesting scenario emerges when the new market is strategically similar to the existing business but the two face serious conflicts. In such a case, it might be better to separate for a period of time and then slowly merge the two concepts so as to minimize the disruption from the conflicts.

Another interesting scenario arises when the new market is fundamentally different from the existing business but the two are not conflicting in a serious way. In such a case, it might be better to first build the new business inside the organization so as to take advantage of the firm's existing assets and experience (and learn about the dynamics of the new market) before separating it into an independent unit.

I describe the four strategies in more detail in the following sections, but bear in mind that deciding when to separate and when to integrate is only part of the solution. It's worth emphasizing the point that some companies have separated the new business model and been successful (such as Singapore Airlines); others have done the same thing and been unsuccessful (such as Continental Airlines). Similarly, some companies integrated the new business model and were successful (such as SMH), while other companies did the same thing and were unsuccessful (such as HMT International). Therefore, having decided which of these strategies to adopt (based on a firm's own circumstances) the key question that must be addressed is, What differentiates the successful firms in each quadrant? I take up this question in Chapter Five.

The Separation Strategy

The bigger the conflicts between the two business models and the lower the possibility that the two models can share synergies, the more appropriate the separation strategy is.

Nestlé and Nespresso. This is the strategy that Nestlé decided to adopt when it set up a separate unit called Nespresso to sell espresso coffee to young urban professionals in the early 1990s. Although the new business involved selling coffee, something for which Nestlé is a market leader, the company's top management decided early on that the similarities between the two businesses were more illusionary than real: whereas Nestlé was selling instant coffee (Nescafé) to the mass market, Nespresso specifically targeted wealthy and young urban professionals and positioned itself as an upmarket brand. Whereas Nestlé sold Nescafé through supermarkets, Nespresso chose an exclusive club to act as its distributor. And whereas Nestlé followed a typical fast-moving consumer goods (FMCG) business model, Nespresso adopted a business model more akin to a luxury goods manufacturer.

Not only were the two business models different, they also conflicted with each other. Nespresso coffee was in effect cannibalizing sales of Nescafé, and the values and attitudes of the young Nespresso organization were the exact opposite of those in the traditional (older) Nestlé organization. For these reasons, Nestlé set up the new unit in a totally different town in Switzerland, assigned one of its rising stars as its CEO, and gave it the freedom and autonomy to compete in its market as it saw fit. The strategy proved to be a great success, and Nespresso is now one of the most profitable units in Nestlé.

HSBC Midland and First Direct. A similar strategy was adopted by HSBC Midland Bank in the United Kingdom when it set up First Direct in the late 1980s—one of the most successful direct (telephone) banks in Europe. According to Graham Picken, the person entrusted with developing First Direct, the decision was made early on to keep the new unit as separate from the established bank as possible so as to minimize conflicts and prevent the parent's existing processes and culture from suffocating the new business model. As he told us,

The question is not whether conflicts exist between the traditional retail banking business and direct banking. They do exist
and are important. The key question is how well the company
manages these conflicts, which will ultimately determine its
success in competing in the two different businesses. Our bank
decided to form First Direct as a stand-alone company and gave
it the freedom to set up its own processes, organizational structure, incentive and control mechanisms, and to create its own
distinct culture. . . . We felt that giving the new unit total autonomy was more important than trying to share resources or cross-
sell to customers. . . . This is an arrangement that worked for
us—it does not mean it would work for others.

The Integration Strategy

Often, the new business model presents few conflicts with the
existing business model of a firm. For example, the Internet
and online distribution of computers was certainly a challenge
for Dell, but the new way of selling computers was not particularly disruptive to Dell's existing business model. In these cases,
embracing the new model through the firm's existing organizational infrastructure may be the optimal strategy. This is especially the case when, in addition to the absence of conflicts, the
two business models serve strategically similar businesses and so
stand to gain from exploiting synergies among them.

Edward Jones & Co. For example, consider again the brokerage
Edward Jones & Co. The firm decided right from the start that it
would not respond to online trading by creating a separate unit.
According to the then managing partner, Doug Hill, the reason was simple: "We have elected not to follow the crowd. We
think online trading is for speculators and entertainment. We are
not in the entertainment business, we are in the 'peace of mind'
business."

How then is Edward Jones responding to the online threat?
By purposely focusing on its established business model and

using the Internet as an opportunity to improve its existing value proposition to its targeted customer. This means looking at the Internet as simply another distribution channel and using it to offer customers better service and more information. Jones's value proposition is face-to-face personal dealings with clients to offer them long-term, conservative investment advice. As a result, the Internet is used not for online trading but as a way of enhancing the brokers' relationship with their customers. As ex-CEO John Bachmann reiterated in a recent article in *Fortune* magazine: "You will not buy securities over the Internet at Edward Jones. That's going to be true as far as I can see into the future. . . . If you aren't interested in a relationship and you just want a transaction, then you could go to E-Trade if you want a good price. We just aren't in that business."[6]

Merrill Lynch. Merrill Lynch is another company that responded to online trading with an integrated strategy. The company launched an online trading channel within the traditional business, adjusting its processes and incentives so that the online business could coexist seamlessly with the existing business. The company developed two new products—Unlimited Advantage and Merrill Lynch Direct—both of which were integrated with the company's existing operations and IT infrastructure. The online products were integrated with the company's existing products so that customers—old or new—could choose from a menu of choices what level of advice they needed and what kind of trading they wanted to undertake. The company's compensation policy was also adjusted so that brokers were now compensated on the value of the total assets they managed, no matter how these assets were acquired (online or via the established network).

The Phased Integration Strategy

It is often the case that the most appropriate strategy is to either separate or integrate the new way of competing *but not right from the start*. For example, when the new business model serves a market that is strategically similar to the existing business but the two ways of competing face serious conflicts between them, the firm faces a difficult challenge: on one hand, it stands to benefit if it integrates the two and exploits their synergies; on the other hand, integration might lead to serious internal problems because of all the conflicts. In such a case, it might be better to separate the two concepts for a period of time and then slowly merge them so as to minimize disruption from the conflicts. This is the *phased integration* strategy.

As with the separation strategy, the challenge that a firm faces in the phased integration strategy is to keep the new business model protected from the mind-sets and policies of the existing business while at the same time trying to exploit synergies between the two businesses. But there is an added complication here: the firm knows that the separation is only temporary and that the new unit will have to be integrated sooner or later with the existing organization. The challenge is to keep the new unit separate but also prepare it for the eventual marriage. Companies can use a number of tactics to achieve this.

Lan & Spar Bank. The Danish bank Lan & Spar is a good example of a company that followed the phased integration strategy. When it decided to set up a direct bank alongside its branch network, it kept the two concepts separate for three years before merging them into one. The CEO, Peter Schou, explained their strategy to me as follows:

> It was a difficult situation to have two concepts at the same time. We couldn't really afford to merge the two concepts from the very beginning because we would have suffered a huge cannibalization cost. Our interest margin at the branch was 10 percent a year whereas at the direct bank it was only 3 percent a year. If we had allowed all of our customers to switch overnight from tradtional banking to direct banking, we would have lost a lot of money. We had to manage the transition carefully.

With eventual consolidation in mind, Lan & Spar separated the direct bank from the rest of the organization but made sure that the IT infrastructure that supported the telephone bank was compatible with the established bank's IT systems. Furthermore, the bank made sure that the employees developed common values and a common culture: employees from both parts of the organization met regularly, attended the same company-wide events, and had similar experiences with the senior managers of the bank. Managers from the main bank were transferred into the direct bank, and the decisions on how to merge the two banks were made in meetings between the managers of both units. The two concepts were finally merged three years after the creation of the direct bank, and all financial indicators suggest that this has been a great success.

Charles Schwab and e.Schwab. Another company that followed the phased integration strategy was Charles Schwab. It had originally set up e.Schwab, its online brokerage business, as a separate unit. But it prepared for eventual integration by having it report directly to then co-CEO David Pottruck and by staffing it with senior managers from the existing retail organization. In addition, e.Schwab's technology platform was designed to integrate with Schwab's IT systems, and the new unit's product and pricing policies were designed to be compatible with the parent's policies. The eventual merger of the two concepts was again judged to be a great success.

The Phased Separation Strategy

When the two business models do not conflict with each other in any serious way but the markets they serve are fundamentally different, the firm faces another interesting challenge: on one hand, given the lack of conflicts, it could integrate the new model with the existing organization without much difficulty.

On the other hand, integration will not bring many benefits and might even constrain the development of the new way of competing into a viable but different business for the firm. In such a case, it might be better to first build the new business inside the organization so as to take advantage of the firm's existing assets and experience (and learn about the dynamics of the new market) before making it an independent unit. This is the *phased separation* strategy. If preparing a unit for marriage is the challenge facing companies that choose the phased integration strategy, the challenge facing companies that choose the phased separation strategy is to prepare a unit for divorce.

Tesco and Tesco.com. This is exactly how Tesco, the United Kingdom's biggest and most successful supermarket chain, is approaching its online distribution arm, Tesco.com. The company's home delivery service was started in the mid-1990s under the name Tesco Direct. The first trials involved one store in west London sending small deliveries to pensioners who couldn't get to the store. The home shopping idea developed over the years, first with customers placing orders from a paper catalog, then from a take-away CD-ROM, and eventually through the company's Web site. By 2000, Tesco's Internet arm was taking 10,000 orders a week, mostly in the Greater London area. By 2003, orders were up to 110,000 per week, and the home delivery service covered all the main stores throughout the United Kingdom.

Over time, the online distribution business developed a life of its own. According to Nick Lansley, the Tesco IT technologies manager:

> We started by offering a narrow range of grocery items, but by the summer of 1996 we wondered why we shouldn't sell every item in a Tesco store online? Why not books and clothes and electronic items? We could either mess about by adding one

product group to another or putting everything on there. We decided to sell everything. It was a huge leap but we felt it was now or never. We weren't worried about competitors. Only Sainsbury was a possible rival and they weren't doing anything that we knew about. But we wondered how to do this? Go to the Board and ask for millions of pounds to build dedicated depots and logistics systems? We looked at other models that we already had developed in-house at Tesco stores.

By 2001, Tesco Direct was reorganized as a full subsidary of Tesco and was renamed Tesco.com—the first step in the divorce proceedings. The online arm redefined its mission from online grocery distribution to online retailer of anything (books, CDs, other nonfood items) and senior managers were hired to lead the new business in the future. In 2003, the Tesco board told Tesco .com management that if everything went well, they planned to spin off the unit as a limited company. The online arm was now such a different business it made little sense to keep it under Tesco management. It had to be given the freedom and autonomy to develop as it saw fit.

According to an analyst in the City of London who covers Tesco, the evolution of Tesco.com into a separate business was understandable:

> Online is seen as a complement to and not a competitor with the traditional offline experience. The online business is allowing Tesco to expand into diversified goods such as CDs and books and is providing additional growth. This diversification is going on in an ad hoc manner. There are obviously teething problems with this development. Buying music or books online at Tesco .com is a very poor experience and is not integrated with the core grocery business. They seem to be experimenting in public view. Why are they doing this? Food online does not provide great margins so they want to expand into higher-margin areas.

What is critical for them is the behavior of consumers—will they prefer to shop for these items in dedicated sites (such as Amazon) or one that provides integrated products and services (that is, Tesco.com)? They are using third-party suppliers for these products (which now include mobile phones and banking services) as a way to minimize inventory risk. They haven't ironed out their going-to-market strategy. This is a big challenge for them. Customers want a seamless shopping experience.

As with the integration strategy, the challenge that firms face in the phased separation strategy is to get the two businesses to exploit any synergies between them while keeping the new business model protected from the existing business. But there is an added twist here: prepare the new unit for eventual separation. As with Tesco, the challenge is how to coexist with something that you know you will divorce eventually.

No Single Best Way

As these examples show, the question that an established firm ought to be asking is not Should we separate the new business model or not? but rather When should we separate it and when should we keep it inside? Under certain circumstances the separation strategy is preferable to the integrated strategy—but under certain other circumstances the integrated strategy might be preferable to separation. Separation is the preferred strategy when the new market is not only strategically different from the existing business but also when the two business models face serious trade-offs and conflicts. On the other hand, no separation is necessary when the new market is very similar to the existing business and presents few conflicts that need managing. In such a case, embracing the new business model through the firm's existing organizational infrastructure is the superior strategy. There are also circumstances that militate toward either eventual merger with an initially separate unit or eventual separation from a unit that started up in-house. Therefore, the best way to tackle this question is by adopting a contingency perspective.

However, as noted earlier, deciding when to separate a unit and when to keep it inside is only part of the solution. Over and above making this decision, what else should a firm do to manage two conflicting business models effectively? I explore this question in Chapter Five.

Summary

- Using dual business models to compete is difficult because of all the conflicts between the two. By trying to pursue business model B, a company harms its business model A.

- The primary solution offered by academics on how to solve this problem is to keep the two business models (and their underlying value chains) physically separate in two distinct organizations. However, this solution has its own cost. It constrains the firm from exploiting potential synergies between the two business models.

- Immediate separation is only one of four possible ways to deal with a second business model. Under certain circumstances the separation strategy is preferable to the integrated strategy, but under certain other circumstances, the integrated strategy might be preferable to separation. There are also circumstances that militate toward either eventual merger with an initially separate unit or eventual separation from a unit that started up in-house.

- The appropriate question to ask is not Should we separate the new business model or not? but rather When should we separate it and when should we keep it inside?

5

SEPARATION IS NOT ENOUGH: HOW TO ACHIEVE AMBIDEXTERITY

Simply separating or integrating the new business model is not enough to ensure success. Four years ago, I undertook a survey of sixty-eight established companies that adopted a second business model in their primary industry (Markides and Charitou, 2004). Seventeen of them were successful, but fifty-one failed to compete successfully with dual business models in operation. Interestingly, of the seventeen successful firms, ten embraced the new business model by creating a separate organizational unit whereas the remaining seven did not. This suggested that separation is not a necessary condition for success—companies could keep the new business model integrated in their existing organizational infrastructure and still succeed. This is a point already emphasized in Chapter Four.

Of more interest for this chapter was the finding that of the sixty-eight firms facing the challenge of dual business models, forty-two created a separate unit and twenty-six did not. And of the forty-two that created a separate unit, only ten were successful. This implied that separation on its own is not enough to ensure success—thirty-two firms (out of forty-two) created a separate unit but still failed!

Consider, for example, the case of IBM. In 1992, in an attempt to compete against low-cost PC clones, IBM launched Ambra—its own clone sold at low prices without overt IBM branding. Ambra was intended to mimic Dell's direct selling model without alienating resellers. At its launch, Ambra president David Middleton claimed that Ambra would capture at least 10 percent of what was then a $10 billion market. IBM management dismissed fears of sales cannibalization, arguing that Ambra personal computers would appeal to a different customer segment than the customers buying IBM-braded PCs.

Yet Ambra turned out to be a classic example of Porter's argument (1980) that a company trying to play a differentiation and low-cost game at the same time will find itself stuck in the middle: prompted by declining sales, a conflicting brand portfolio, and an overburdened cost structure, IBM closed Ambra in 1994. IBM's failure to compete in two business models simultaneously stands in stark contrast to the success of several other companies who have done exactly that with great success. Companies such as Toyota (with its Lexus car), Intel (with its low-cost Celeron chip), SMH (with its Swatch brand) and Nestlé (with its Nespresso subsidiary) are all examples of organizations that have found ways to manage two business models successfully through separate units. Why did these companies succeed when IBM failed?

Consider also the case of the airline industry. Singapore Airlines appears to have succeeded in competing in the low-end, point-to-point segment of the airline market through the establishment of a low-cost subsidiary, originally named Tradewinds but renamed Silkair in 1992. However, companies such as Continental Airlines, British Airways, and KLM have failed to crack this market despite setting up separate subsidiaries to do so (Continental Lite, GO, and Buzz, respectively). Why the difference in outcomes?

What explains the different fortunes of these companies in using dual business models? Surely the difference is not the fact that some firms (that is, the successful ones) keep the new business model in a separate unit and others (the unsuccessful ones) do not! British Airways and KLM created separate units but did not have much success in doing so. On the other hand, Lan & Spar Bank in Denmark succeeded in dual business models despite keeping the second business model inside the existing organization.

Achieving Ambidexterity

Over and above deciding to separate or integrate the new business model, an established firm needs to decide how to manage it once the separation-integration decision has been made. If the preferred strategy is *separation*, the company must still find ways to exploit its existing strengths (such as its brand name, financial resources, and industry experience) in the new unit without constraining it. Similarly, if the preferred strategy is *integration*, the company must still strive to protect the new business model from excessive interference or mismanagement by the parent, all in the name of exploiting synergies.

Separate but Exploit Synergies

The key to a successful separation strategy is to protect the new business model in a separate unit but not give up on synergies altogether. Despite knowing that the two businesses are strategically dissimilar and that there is little scope for exploiting synergies, companies must still put in place processes and mechanisms to exploit any synergies whenever they arise. Obviously, the potential for synergies varies by company (depending on how strategically similar the two markets are). This means that the level of integration needed varies by company as well. As a result, different companies must put in place different levels of integrating mechanisms. But the important point to note is that to be successful, companies must always find ways to exploit synergies, no matter how small or limited they are.

This key point is consistent with the work of Lawrence and Lorsch (1967) on how companies achieve integration and differentiation simultaneously. In their seminal study, they found that compared to unsuccessful companies, successful ones were able to achieve high degrees of both integration and differentiation. They also found that the level of differentiation needed in each firm was a function of the external environment facing the firm (dynamic environments require more differentiation). This meant that firms operating in dynamic environments had to be highly differentiated, a condition that would make it more difficult to maintain the required state of integration. On the other hand, firms operating in stable environments could achieve the appropriate level of integration more easily. All this meant that successful firms used a different combination of devices for achieving integration: the firms in dynamic environments used more integrating devices (and more elaborate ones) than the firms in stable environments. But both sets of firms used integrating devices, no matter how small the need for integration was.

This is exactly what I am proposing here—and exactly what I found in my survey of sixty-eight firms that attempted to compete with dual business models. Consider, for example, the forty-two sample firms that separated the new business model into an independent unit. As reported earlier, ten were successful and thirty-two unsuccessful. Using multiple regression analysis to identify the determinants of success, I found the following results (see Table 5.1):

- On average, the higher the degree of autonomy that corporate headquarters gave the new unit to make *financial* and *operational* decisions, the more effective the firm was in managing the two business models.
- On average, the more differentiated the budgetary and investment policies of the new unit relative to the parent, the more effective the firm was in managing both business models next to each other.
- On average, firms were less effective in using two business models when they adopted different evaluation and incentive systems in the new unit (compared to the established business).
- On average, firms that assigned an insider to be CEO of the new unit were more effective than firms that used outsiders.

Table 5.1.   Administrative Mechanisms in the Firms That Created a Separate Unit.

Administrative Mechanism (scale)	Successful Firms (10)	Unsuccessful Firms (32)
Strategic autonomy (1–5)	3.0	3.2
Financial autonomy (1–5)	4.1	2.9
Operational autonomy (1–5)	4.4	3.1
Different culture (1–6)	4.6	4.0
Different budgetary policies (1–6)	4.5	3.9
Different incentive systems (1–6)	3.2	3.6
Different rewards (1–6)	3.2	3.2
Has a new CEO been appointed specifically for the unit or not? (0–1)	0.8	0.6
CEO from inside (0–1)	0.8	0.6

Note: Autonomy is measured on a scale of 1 to 5, with 1 being "no autonomy to the separate unit" and 5 being "the unit makes all decisions." Other variables are measured on a 1 to 6 scale, with 1 meaning that the policies between the main business and the unit are very similar and 6 being very different. (CEO appointment is measured on a zero-to-one scale.)

- On average, firms that allowed the new unit to develop its own culture were more effective in managing the new business model next to the established one than firms that expected the new unit to adopt the corporate culture.

What these results suggest is that successful firms give much more operational and financial autonomy to their units than unsuccessful firms do. They also allow the units to develop their own cultures and budgetary systems and to have their own CEO. These are all policies consistent with the notion that the new units need freedom to operate as they see fit in their own environment. Note, however, that this autonomy did not come at the expense of synergies: the parent still kept close watch over the strategy of the unit, and cooperation between the unit and the parent was encouraged through common incentive and reward systems. In addition, the CEO of the units was transferred from inside the organization so as to facilitate closer cooperation and active exploitation of synergies.

These survey results were further supported by personal statements from senior managers who faced the challenge of managing two business models. For example, a senior executive at a major U.S. office supplies firm commented as follows:

> I refused to have a P&L for the dot-com operation and a different P&L for the main business. This could only have created frictions and political infighting. All the VPs are measured on our consolidated sales, not the sales of the parent versus the unit. And no matter what method the customer uses to place an order [phone, Internet, store], the salesperson responsible for the region will get the credit for it.

Similarly, the strategy director of a major European airline company suggested the following:

> It makes absolutely no sense to create a separate low-cost subsidiary and not give it the freedom to decide what to do in its market. But it is equally silly to ignore that we have been in the airline business for more than half a century. Surely our subsidiary can learn something from us!

To summarize: separation is neither necessary nor sufficient to ensure success. Even if a firm decides to separate the new business model, it must still find ways to exploit its existing strengths (such as its brand name, financial resources, and industry experience) in the new unit. In this sense, the question that needs to be asked is not Should we separate or not? but rather What activities in our value chain do we separate and what activities do we keep integrated?[1]

Integrate but Avoid Conflicts

As with the separation strategy just described, simply integrating the new way of competing into the existing infrastructure is not enough to ensure success. The most successful firms are those that not only integrate the new business model but *also treat the new way of competing as a wonderful new opportunity to grow the business*. This not only allows them to learn from the new ways of competing and incorporate this learning into their existing business, it also encourages people to develop a protective attitude toward the new business model and so take extreme care not to suffocate it with the existing policies of the firm. A good example of this is Merrill Lynch's decision to change its incentive systems so that its brokers would have an incentive to support online trading.

Treating the new business model as an opportunity rather than as a threat is very important. Categorization theory argues that framing an external development as an opportunity increases involvement in the process of resolving it, participation at lower levels of the organization, and actions directed at changing the external environment.[2] In their study of how U.S. newspaper companies responded to the Internet, Clark Gilbert and Joe Bower (2002) made a similar point. They argued that when an organization first confronts a conflicting business model, it's better to look at it as a threat rather than as an opportunity. Framing it as a threat will generate serious commitment in the organization to respond to the threat aggressively. However, when the organization is actually ready *to create a new business model* to exploit the new market, it's better to look at it as an opportunity. This way, old models and assumptions will be set aside and the new business model will be evaluated on its own merits. According to Gilbert and Bower, recognizing the need to simultaneously manage competing frames is the key to effective response.

Viewing the new business model as an opportunity will not only free the minds of managers from the economics and realities of the established business but will also encourage entrepreneurial behaviors from everybody in the organization. It will also determine how aggressively the company approaches the new way of competing and how persistently its people pursue it—despite early setbacks.

Consider, for example, the following two quotes from senior managers at two U.S. firms that were part of my survey. The first is VP at a major office supplies firm. His company approached Internet distribution as an opportunity to be aggressively exploited, and the company did so with great success:

> We got onto the Internet long before anybody else knew what the Internet was. In fact, our biggest problem for the first two years was persuading our *customers* to use it! But we persisted because I knew in my bones that the Internet was *it*. This new technology was going to be the future. It would be the medium that would allow us to do great new things.

The second quote is from the CEO of a major bookseller. His company did not consider the online distribution of books as a particularly attractive way of doing business, and its response turned out to be hugely unprofitable and in the end unsuccessful:

> We were late in implementing [it] but not in evaluating it. And our evaluation was that this thing did not make sense. Yet every time I tried to explain our reasons why we wouldn't do it to Wall Street, my share price went down! Even in 1997 when online distribution of books went from zero to 6 percent, superstores increased their share from 10 percent to 22 percent—yet our stock price dropped by 40 percent. So in the end, we decided we had to do something.

Treating the new business model as an opportunity rather than as a threat has some additional advantages. By looking at it as an opportunity, the firm approaches the task in a proactive, strategic manner rather than as a hasty knee-jerk reaction to a problem. The new market is evaluated in a reasoned and deliberate way, and necessary resources are allocated to exploit (and grow) the opportunity. More important, the most respected managers in the organization are assigned to the task and the project receives high-level attention and care. Finally, looking at it as an opportunity encourages the firm to take a long-term view on the investment. This ensures resources and long-term commitment even when the initial results are not encouraging.

Of all the advantages associated with treating the new business model as an opportunity, perhaps the most important one is that it allows managers to put old mental models and assumptions aside and approach the opportunity in a creative and entrepreneurial way. This in turn allows them to put in place innovative strategies that take advantage of the opportunity without undermining the established business.

To understand how a firm can do this, it is important to remember that often (but not always) new business models create markets that have much lower margins than the traditional markets. This suggests that even in the best-case scenario—when an established company is thoroughly successful in embracing the new model—the end result will be cannibalization of existing sales and much lower margins! Consider, for example, the following comment from a VP at a major fast-moving consumer goods company:

> The issue is not whether we can respond to the private label threat successfully. I believe we can do it, either internally or through a separate unit. But what is the purpose of doing this if the end result is to destroy the industry? I don't want to play *their* game. What we need to do is to find a response that builds on our competencies and restores the margins in this business.

The logic of this argument was echoed in another comment that an SMH executive offered to explain the reasoning behind the development of the Swatch back in the early 1980s:

> We had to defend the low end of the market against cheap Japanese watches. But we did not want to simply compete on price. . . . We had to find a way of producing something that was *cheap enough* [emphasis added] but was still Swiss quality.

Both of these comments point to what I believe is the key to the success of the companies that choose the integration strategy: embracing the new business model in a creative way that builds upon the competences of the established competitors and also restores the margins in the business to a higher level than what the new business model offers.

SMH and Swatch

Consider, for example, the SMH Swatch story again. In the early 1960s, the Swiss dominated the global watch industry. This dominance all but evaporated in the 1970s when companies such as Seiko (from Japan) and Timex (from the United States) introduced cheap watches that used quartz technology and provided added functionality and features (such as the alarm function, date indication, and so on). Swiss share of global world production declined from 48 percent in 1965 to 15 percent by 1980. In response, the Swiss introduced the Swatch. Not only did the new watch introduce style as a competitive dimension, it sold at a price that was on average three times higher than the average Seiko price. Since its launch in 1983, Swatch has become the world's most popular timepiece with more than 100 million sold in more than thirty countries.

The secret of this success lies in two areas. First, note that the established competitors (the Swiss) were selling their product on the basis of performance when they suddenly came under attack from the new business model. The attack took the form of "Our watches are good enough in performance and superior to the Swiss in price." What the Swiss did was to turn this rationale on its head. They sold their Swatch on the following premise: "Our watches are good enough in price and superior to the Japanese in performance (that is, style)." This sounds easy but it requires a fundamental (dare I say revolutionary) change in mind-set!

Instead of adopting the mind-set that said, "Minimize price subject to a performance level that is good enough," the new mind-set needed is one that says, "Maximize performance subject to a price that is good enough."

And it's one thing to say this and another to do it. In effect, what the Swiss did was to produce something that delivered low cost *and* differentiation at the same time—managing two conflicting business models simultaneously. They achieved this by eliminating many product attributes they thought were unnecessary (thus cutting costs) while enhancing certain other product features like style and design (thus building differentiation). They also found ways to cut other costs (in manufacturing and in materials used) and to build differentiation in other ways (for example, through the Swatch Club). The end result was a strategy that embraced the key features of the new business model in a creative way without abandoning traditional Swiss values and competences.

Gillette

Another example of the same strategy is Gillette's response to the disposable razor threat. Disposables entered the razor market on the premise, "Our products are good enough in performance and superior to Gillette in price." How did Gillette choose to adopt the new business model embodied by the disposables? By building on the premise, "Our disposables are good enough in price and superior to other disposables in performance."

Rather than debate whether to manufacture a cheaper disposable or not, Gillette chose to tackle the new business model in a creative manner. By adopting the mind-set, "We need to maximize performance subject to a price that is good enough," Gillette designers developed a number of innovative disposable products that competed not on price but on performance. For example, in 1994 they introduced the Custom Plus line, a disposable with a lubricating strip. In late 2002, they announced the introduction of a new line of disposable razors with proprietary technology—a disposable version of the triple-blade razor, the company's premier product in refillables. By successfully adopting the low-cost *and* differentiation strategies at the same time, Gillette managed to maintain a 45 percent market share in disposables.

The lesson from these success stories is simple: it *is* possible to manage two conflicting business models without keeping them apart. But to do so requires creativity and a willingness to go beyond simply imitating a new business model. By focusing only on finding ways to accommodate a new model so as to minimize potential conflicts, established companies may be missing an opportunity to exploit the new model in ways that build on their unique competences and restore their markets to higher levels of profitability.

Note that saying that companies such as Swatch and Gillette adopted a low-cost and differentiation strategy does not suggest that they were the best differentiator and the cost leader at the same time! The key thing to remember here is that both Swatch and Gillette stuck to their basis of competitive advantage (differentiation) but found a way to do it better (at a lower cost). They did *not* adopt a cost leader's strategy, which is based on skills in the manufacturing process, and therefore chose not to compete head-on with the low-cost players (where they would no doubt lose). Instead, they built their new strategy on unique design and marketing skills, playing the game differently from their competitors.

A Framework for Ambidexterity

The discussion thus far suggests that in deciding how to operate two conflicting business models simultaneously, a company ought to go through a decision-making process that involves three steps:

- First, ask, "Should we adopt the new business model or not?" The answer to this question depends on the specific circumstances of each firm.
- If the decision is made that the firm ought to adopt the new business model, the second question that must be asked is "Should we separate or integrate the new business model or should we follow one of the phased strategies?" The answer to this question will most likely depend on the two key variables identified in Chapter Four, the ones that define the axes of Figure 4.1.
- Finally, once the separation-integration decision is made, the question arises: "Given our choice, how could we manage the new unit successfully?"

This chapter focuses on the last question, identifying several variables that could influence how well a second business model is managed in each of the four quadrants of Figure 4.1. For example, I argue that companies that adopt the *separation* strategy will do better if they

- Give operational and financial autonomy to their new unit but still maintain close watch over the strategy of the unit and encourage cooperation between the unit and the parent through common incentive and reward systems.
- Allow the unit to develop its own culture and budgetary system.

- Allow the unit to have a CEO of its own, someone who is transferred from inside the organization (and not a newly hired outsider).

Similarly, I have found that companies that adopt the *integration* strategy will do better if they

- Treat the new business model as a wonderful new opportunity to grow the business (rather than see it as a threat).
- Apply the strengths of the traditional business to find ways to differentiate themselves (rather than imitating the strategies of their attackers).
- Approach the task in a proactive, strategic manner rather than as a hasty knee-jerk reaction to a problem.
- Take extreme care not to suffocate the new business with the existing policies of the firm.

It is important to stress two key points at this juncture. First, notwithstanding the success stories described in this chapter, large-sample results also show that simultaneously pursuing two business models that have inherent conflicts is extremely problematic and will, *on average*, fail. Here, I have focused on the outliers. Companies that are considering whether to adopt a second business model or not ought to keep in mind that the odds are still against them. But as the study of outliers in this chapter suggests, the rewards from a nuanced approach to competing with dual business models can be great.

Second and more important, this chapter has identified only a few of the things that companies ought to do to operate dual business models successfully. Other researchers have explored the same issue and, as a result, the list of ideas and advice on what companies ought to do has grown quite long. The box lists thirty ideas that have been developed in the last few years alone!

What Else to Do Over and Above Creating a Separate Unit

- Employ a common general manager between the main and the new business (O'Reilly and Tushman, 2004).
- Allow different cultures to emerge but unite the two with a strong shared vision (O'Reilly and Tushman, 2004).
- Use targeted (limited) integrative mechanisms (O'Reilly and Tushman, 2004).
- Staff the new business model with ambidextrous individuals (Birkinshaw and Gibson, 2004).
- Legitimize diverse perspectives and capabilities (Bartlett and Ghoshal, 1989).
- Build strong shared values that unite the people in the two businesses (Bartlett and Ghoshal, 1989).
- Do everything to avoid a silo mentality (for example, transfer of people, common conferences, rituals (Bartlett and Ghoshal, 1989).
- Frame it as both a threat and an opportunity (Gilbert and Bower, 2002).
- Fund it in stages (Gilbert and Bower, 2002).
- Cultivate outside perspectives by hiring new people for the separate unit (Gilbert, 2003; Gilbert and Bower, 2002).
- Appoint an active and credible integrator (Gilbert and Bower, 2002).
- Emphasize "soft" levers such as a strong sense of direction, strong values, a feeling of "we are in this together" (Ghoshal and Gratton, 2003).
- Develop incentives that encourage cooperation between the two (Ghoshal and Gratton, 2003).
- Identify measurement and evaluation metrics specific to the unit (Govindarajan and Trimble, 2005b).
- Hire outsiders to run the unit with a mixture of insiders (Govindarajan and Trimble, 2005a).

- Be patient for revenues but impatient for profits (Christensen and Raynor, 2003).
- Integrate the activities that cannot be done well if they become independent (Christensen and Raynor, 2003).
- Allow the unit to borrow brand name, physical assets, expertise, and useful processes (Govindarajan and Trimble, 2005b).
- Give the unit enough power to fight in its own corner (Govindarajan and Trimble, 2005b).
- Ensure adequate flow of information through transfer of people and the intranet (Day, Mang, Richter, and Roberts, 2001).
- Develop a culture of openness (Day and others, 2001).
- Insulate the unit but don't isolate it (Harreld, 2004).
- Develop strong shared values and strong culture (Tushman and O'Reilly, 1996).
- Make sure an independent executive from outside the business unit secures an internal champion to manage the unit and provides oversight (Day and others, 2001).
- Give the new unit operational autonomy but exercise strong central strategic control (Markides and Charitou, 2004).
- Allow the unit to develop its own strategy, without even thinking about the existing business (Markides and Charitou, 2004).
- Think of phased integration (Iansiti, McFarlan, and Westerman, 2003).
- Give the unit autonomy but don't lose control (Markides and Charitou, 2004).
- Allow the unit to differentiate itself by adopting a few of its own value-chain activities but at the same time exploit synergies by ensuring that some value-chain activities are shared (Markides and Charitou, 2004).
- Evaluate the unit subjectively (Govindarajan and Trimble, 2005a).

From Tactics to a Framework

Rather than provide laundry lists of things that companies could do to achieve ambidexterity (that is, to manage two business models simultaneously), it may be better to develop a way of thinking about it. Every company could then apply this way of thinking to its specific circumstances. How, then, should managers think about the challenge of *achieving ambidextrous behaviors* in their organizations?

Over the past few years, executives throughout the world have been exposed to a fascinating game developed by professors Jay Forrester and John Sterman at MIT. Originally known as the "Production-Distribution Game," it is now more popularly known as the "Beer Game." The game is played on a board that represents the production and distribution of beer.[3] The main objective of the game is to make participants appreciate that the underlying structure of the Beer Game creates the behavior they observe in the game, and that behavior will change only with changes in the underlying structure in the game.

This result has immediate applicability in real-life company situations: the behaviors observed in any company are created by the underlying structure or underlying organizational environment that exists in that company, and those behaviors will only change if people first change the underlying environment. Therefore, if for whatever reason you do not consider the behavior you observe in your company to be optimal, the first thing to do is *not* to complain about it or blame people—rather, focus on changing the underlying environment of the organization. Behaviors such as innovation, trust, customer orientation, and the like do not occur simply because leaders ask for them; it is necessary to create the appropriate organizational environment for the desired behavior to emerge.[4]

By organizational environment, I mean four basic elements: the *culture of the company*, which includes its norms, values, and unquestioned assumptions; the *structure of the company*, comprising not only its formal hierarchy but also its physical setup as well as its systems (information, recruitment, market research, and the like); the *incentives in the company*, both monetary and nonmonetary; and finally, *the company's people*, including their skills and attributes (see Figure 5.1). It is the combination of these four elements that creates the organizational environment that in turn supports and promotes the behavior desired in a company.

The Environment for Ambidexterity

This suggests that to develop an organization capable of operating dual and conflicting business models (that is, an ambidextrous organization), it is first necessary to ask and answer the question, What kind of culture, structures, incentives, and people do we need to put in place in our organization to promote and encourage ambidextrous behaviors on the part of our employees?

Figure 5.1.   The Underlying Organizational Environment That Determines Behaviors in a Firm.

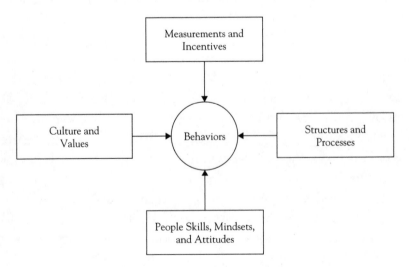

This question has many possible answers, and even the long list just given highlights only a few of them. Consider, for example, the French supermarket chain E. Leclerc.

E. Leclerc

Leclerc was founded in the late 1950s by Eduard Leclerc, who decided to give up a career as a Catholic priest and start a supermarket dedicated to offering branded products at cheap prices. The organization has been very successful and has grown to a chain of more than five hundred hypermarkets. It is now expanding overseas.

This organization balances quite a few conflicting forces smoothly: it has achieved low cost and differentiation simultaneously; it is very decentralized and yet centralized at the same time; it is broken up into many small autonomous units but still enjoys the benefits of size; it is structured as a federation of independent stores yet behaves as an integrated network; it encourages continuous experimentation with new products and concepts yet survives the inevitable losses without pain; its employees feel and behave like owners of the organization, yet own no stock; the whole organization behaves like one big family, yet it is a money-making machine. How could it possibly achieve all these things simultaneously and how does it manage such variety?

The answer to this question has many angles. First of all, Leclerc is not a single company. Each store is owned and operated by individuals who choose to trade under the Leclerc name. But they are not franchisees either: they do not have to pay for the right to trade under the Leclerc name (indeed, they receive numerous other benefits from their Leclerc association, for which they do not have to pay anything). However, they have to agree to abide by certain norms and regulations—the primary one being that they will never be undersold by competitors. In addition, no one—not even a member of the Leclerc family—is allowed to own more than two stores.

Each store is given total autonomy over its affairs. For example, given its unique geographical location and consumer mix, each store is free to decide what products to sell, what prices to charge, what promotions to run, and so on. In addition, each store can find its own suppliers and negotiate its own prices. All this decentralization and autonomy encourages experimentation and achieves differentiation. But this differentiation is not achieved at the expense of low cost: for example, each region has its own regional warehouse (owned by the member stores). The warehouse orders and stores those types of products that do not need to be sold fresh. This achieves purchasing economies. In addition, a central purchasing department in Paris identifies potential suppliers and negotiates prices with them. Individual stores do not have to agree to any supplier recommended by the center, but this method certainly achieves purchasing economies. The use of the Leclerc name by all also achieves advertising and promotional benefits and cuts costs. Finally, new Leclerc stores are always started by current Leclerc employees who receive the financial backing and guarantees of current Leclerc store owners. The financial backing of a prominent local businessperson has inevitable benefits in dealing with banks for start-up capital.

In addition to all this, every store owner is active in the management of the whole organization. They all attend monthly regional meetings as well as frequent national meetings where decisions are taken and experiences exchanged. Stores belong to regions and each region is run by a member for three years (on a voluntary basis, of course). Not only do the region presidents run the affairs of their regions, they also travel extensively to individual stores to offer advice, monitor plans, and transfer best practice. Furthermore, at the end of every year, the store owners each must distribute 25 percent of their store's profits to their employees. They also have the *duty* (not obligation) to act as a "godparent" to one of their employees. The selected employee is someone who has been identified as having high potential and being a possible future Leclerc store owner. This individual receives continuous support and advice—and (when the time comes) financial backing and moral support to start a new store. If that store fails, the "godparent" is financially liable for any debts.

How is so much variety managed? Information systems are definitely used to monitor what is happening across the federation. Frequent meetings also help exchange ideas and monitor progress. However, the two primary mechanisms of control are a common and deeply felt vision that sets the parameters within which each member store operates, and a strong family culture where everybody is treated with fairness and openness and where everybody is equal. It is interesting that each store has its own unique culture (created primarily by the personality of the store owner), yet a common Leclerc culture still permeates the whole organization. This common culture sets the parameters, the accepted norms, the shared values, and the constraints within which individuals behave. It is this shared culture that allows so much autonomy and freedom without the fear that somebody, somewhere, will do something nasty.

So, how did Leclerc achieve such ambidexterity? Part of the answer lies in its strong vision and culture. Part of it is in its strong shared values. A lot has to do with the kind of individuals being recruited and promoted in such a system. And some of it has to do with the structures and processes that have been put in place. In short, ambidexterity is achieved because the total "organizational environment" of Leclerc has been designed to promote ambidextrous behaviors by everybody in the organization.

Summary

- Simply protecting the new business model in a separate unit, away from the main business, is not enough to ensure success. The company must still create *ambidexterity*, that is, it must find ways to exploit synergies between the unit and the parent organization.

- Such ambidexterity can only be achieved if the company puts in place the appropriate "organizational environment" (that is, culture, structure, incentives, and people) that promotes ambidextrous behaviors.

- Whether the new business model is put in a separate unit or integrated into the existing structure, the company must treat the new way of competing as an opportunity rather than as a threat.

6

RESPONDING TO
BUSINESS-MODEL INNOVATION

The evidence shows that business-model innovation is often pioneered by start-up firms and new entrants rather than by the established players in an industry. For example, it was not the established airline companies that introduced the low-cost, no-frills way of flying in the industry—it was newcomers such as Southwest, Ryanair, and easyJet. Similarly, it was not the established booksellers that introduced online bookselling as a way of competing in the industry—it was newcomers Charles Stack (an Ohio-based firm) and Amazon.

To understand why that is the case, it is enough to reflect on the characteristics of business-model innovations that I presented in Chapter One. As noted, this kind of innovation displays the following characteristics:

- At least initially, it is of no interest to the customers of the established firms (who want a different value proposition from the one offered by the innovator, and who will say so if asked). As a result, established firms would have few incentives to push for it (Christensen, 1997).
- It requires a different combination of tailored activities (value chain as well as culture, structures, and incentives) from the ones that the established firm already has in place.
- It requires a set of activities that not only differ from but often conflict with the activities that the established firm uses in its established business.

- It creates new markets that at least initially start out as small and insignificant relative to the established business.

- It creates new markets that require a long period of investment before turning profitable, making them unappealing to today's impatient capital.

- It not only expands existing markets but also cannibalizes customers of the established firms, so these firms tend to view it as more threat than opportunity (Gilbert, 2003; Gilbert and Bower, 2002).

Given these characteristics, it should not come as a surprise to know that most established companies will tend to shy away from business-model innovation. To begin with, these innovations are of no interest to their mainstream customers. To make matters worse, they (often) start life as small and unprofitable niches. And to top it all off, they have the potential of eating into their existing (profitable) business. All this means that business-model innovation is not high on the priority list of established firms. It also means that one of the major challenges that established firms face is how to respond to this kind of innovation if somebody else introduces it in their markets.

How then could an established firm respond to invading business models? Unfortunately, the word *respond* has become synonymous for many firms with "imitate the innovation." It is not unusual to hear established firms complain about the disruption created in their markets by an invading business model and then follow that complaint with the question: Should I also do this or not? And how can I do it without harming my existing business? Thus, the debate within established brokers has long been about whether to get into online brokerage or not. Similarly, the debate within established airline companies has often been about getting into the low-cost, no-frills part of the business or not. It's as if the only available response to an invading business model is to either ignore it or imitate it!

Needless to say, other responses to business-model innovation are possible. Adopting the new business model is certainly one way to respond, but it's not the only one. How then could incumbents respond to such disruptive innovation? And when do they do what? This chapter explores these questions in more detail.

Response One: Focus on My Business Model

One of the biggest misconceptions about business-model innovation is that the new way of doing things is sure to grow and eventually overtake the traditional way of competing in the market. As a result, established competitors have been encouraged to face up to the innovation by embracing it in some form or another. This misconception probably arose from research on technological innovation, where new technologies did completely replace existing technologies, in the process destroying competitors who did not make the jump from the old to the new. This may be generally true for technological innovations, but it is certainly not the case for most business-model innovations.

More often than not, the new way of competing creates a new market on the periphery of the established market. The new market is originally composed of entirely new customers who get attracted by the new value proposition offered by the invading business model. Over time, customers from the established market find the new value proposition attractive as well, and the newly created market grows quickly. However, even when the new market grows at the expense of the established one, it never destroys the established market completely. Some customers always prefer the value proposition offered by the established players and, as a result, do not defect to the new market.

What this simple fact implies is that an established competitor does not necessarily have to adopt the new way. Because the new way of competing is creating a new market while at the same time encroaching on the established market, the incumbent cannot ignore it—it should respond to it. But it could respond to the innovation not by adopting it but by investing in its existing business to make the traditional way of competing more competitive relative to the new way of competing. This might sound like an obvious point, but most established competitors seem to ignore it.

Yet this is exactly what Gillette did in the face of the disposable razor threat. Like all other business-model innovations, disposables entered the razor market by emphasizing a different value proposition for the product—in this case, price and ease of use versus Gillette's closeness of shave. This allowed them to grow quickly and claim a large segment of the market in a short time. How did Gillette respond to the new way of competing? Without completely ignoring disposables, Gillette chose to focus most of its resources on its traditional business to improve its competitive standing relative to the new way of doing business. It produced disposable razors in a defensive way but focused its energy and resources on its main business and innovated by creating two new products, the Sensor and the Mach-3. Even Gillette's November 2002 decision to create a new line of disposables did not come at the expense of its main business. Innovation in the traditional business eventually led to the decline of the disposable razor market from the heights of the 1970s.

Responding to the innovation by not imitating it but by investing in the traditional way of competing is a valid response to the threat. In a survey I undertook in 2002 on how incumbents responded to invading business-model innovations, I asked firms to tell me the reasons that led them to *not* adopt the new business model. As illustrated in Figure 6.1, the most important reason for not embracing it was the established firms' desire to remain focused on their existing business. Another important factor was the fact that these companies had invested a lot in their business and therefore wanted to capitalize on their investment. Figure 6.1 lists an array of factors that affected the decision not to embrace the newly created business model.

Figure 6.1.   Factors Affecting Decision Not to Embrace the New Business Model.

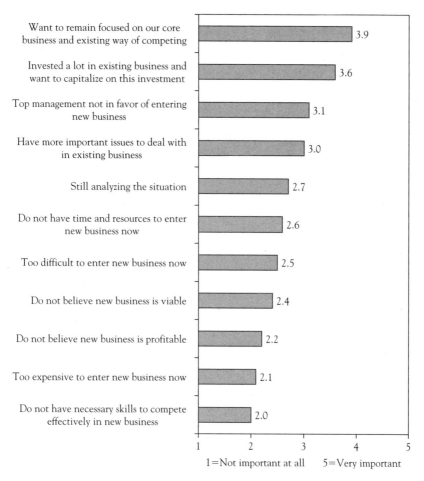

Want to remain focused on our core business and existing way of competing	3.9
Invested a lot in existing business and want to capitalize on this investment	3.6
Top management not in favor of entering new business	3.1
Have more important issues to deal with in existing business	3.0
Still analyzing the situation	2.7
Do not have time and resources to enter new business now	2.6
Too difficult to enter new business now	2.5
Do not believe new business is viable	2.4
Do not believe new business is profitable	2.2
Too expensive to enter new business now	2.1
Do not have necessary skills to compete effectively in new business	2.0

1=Not important at all   5=Very important

The broker Edward Jones & Co. is one of the companies that decided not to embrace the innovation (that is, Internet brokerage) that invaded their market in the mid-1990s. According to John Bachmann, the firm's managing partner at the time, the reason for this was simple:

> The past few years have been kind to "do-it-yourself" investors. But people forget that the market can also go down. Many of these investors will suffer when the market turns sour. Our

strategy of providing personal, face-to-face advice to investors will be attractive in a down market—in fact, it may be especially so. Our system will show its true value to the customer in a downturn. Edward Jones serves as a "shock absorber" for the end consumer. Customers come to us for advice. This advice will be especially useful in bad times.

How then did Edward Jones respond to the arrival of online trading? By purposely focusing on its established way of playing the game and improving its own value proposition for its targeted customer. Instead of embracing online brokerage trading, Edward Jones invested its resources and energy on extending its network of branch offices across the country, increasing the number of brokers, and improving its personal, face-to-face service to individual investors. The company's one-person office strategy runs counter to that of virtually every other major securities firm in the United States, and has helped fuel remarkable growth: the number of Edward Jones offices has expanded from a total of 304 in 1980 to more than 8,000 today (more than any other brokerage firm in the country).

Jones's trademarks of single-broker offices, emphasis on personal relationships, face-to-face dealings with clients, and conservative style of managing assets remain unchanged despite the emergence and rapid expansion of online trading. The company's brokers continue to provide this personal brand of service by discussing their clients' individual investment needs on a one-to-one basis. Foremost among the values these brokers have in common is that their job is to offer sound, long-term financial advice to customers, even if that advice does not generate short-term fees for the brokers. The Jones philosophy, that service to the individual is of utmost importance, is ingrained in every single broker working in the Jones system. This customer-first value is a major reason why the company did not embrace the new online trading business and does not intend to do so in the future.

The Gillette and Edward Jones examples demonstrate that reinvesting in your own value proposition and improving your own business model is a valid way to respond to an invading business model. The key to success is to improve the established value proposition *without ignoring* the value proposition of the invading business model. Specifically, for this strategy to work, the established firm must reach a point where it could legitimately say: "I am good enough in the value proposition of the invading business model *and* superior in my own value proposition." Note that the established firm must not only improve its own value proposition but must also adopt some of the elements of the new value proposition as well. It cannot afford to totally ignore what the business-model innovation is bringing into the market.

Such a strategy is not without risks. The biggest mistake that a company could make is to keep improving its value proposition to a degree that its customers do not really want or value. The second biggest mistake is to improve its value proposition without investing to make it good enough in what the innovators are offering. Therefore, before embarking on the focus strategy, a firm must ask three questions:

- Am I improving my value proposition in ways that customers would value? (And not simply overengineering my offering.)
- Is there really a market for my current value proposition? (And not attempting to shore up a market in terminal decline.)
- Can I honestly claim that my value proposition is good enough in the product attributes that the innovator's value proposition is emphasizing? (In addition to being superior to it in the product attributes that I am emphasizing.)

It's only when the established firm can answer these questions in a satisfactory manner that the focus strategy could be adopted as a response to the invading business model.

Response Two: Ignore It—"This Is Not My Business"

One other firm that chose not to respond to the business-model innovation introduced in its industry is U.S.-based Hartford Life Insurance Co. In explaining why his company did not embrace the new way of selling life and health insurance in a direct (phone or Internet) way, the director of marketing for individual life products argued as follows:

> We currently target the top 5 percent of affluent Americans. Typically, these people have a net worth in excess of $2 million. This target market has complex financial problems, and as a result, often needs professional advisers to identify problems and solutions. The life insurance agent or broker, working with the client's attorney or accountant, is often used to provide this consultation as part of the selling process. People with lower income levels do not have such complex financial issues and may be more approachable through direct sales methods. Since this is not our target market, and our product and distribution does not focus on this market, we do not see direct sales as a current threat, nor do we see it as a sales opportunity. The financials of [the direct] market are quite different from the one we target. Therefore, we have spent little resources on evaluating or implementing direct marketing strategies. The affluent market is large, and growing fast enough to fuel our growth for the foreseeable future.

The experience of Hartford Life Insurance Co. highlights an important characteristic of business-model innovation that could easily lead established companies astray: the markets created by business-model innovations may *appear* to be simple extensions of the main market while they are in fact miles away. For example, is the replacement car rental market created by Enterprise Rent-A-Car related to the airport car rental market where Hertz operates, or are the two markets totally different? Is online brokerage similar to traditional brokerage or a totally different industry? Is the budget airline market an extension of the main airline market, or are the two markets unrelated for all practical purposes? The truth of the matter is that very often, the new markets created by the innovation require such different skills and mind-sets from what the established firms use (and need) in their main markets that moving into the new market can be nothing more than unrelated diversification for the established firm. In such cases, the firm may be better off by simply ignoring the new business model.

This sentiment was expressed clearly by a director of Commercial & General Union insurance company in the United Kingdom. In defending his firm's decision not to embrace the new direct insurance business, he argued that it is difficult for established companies to experiment with major new projects such as direct insurance, as these projects deviate significantly from the traditional way of doing business and thereby entail high risks and unclear benefits. As he put it: "It's like trying to test whether a nuclear bomb can destroy London! Some ideas are just too big for established companies to experiment with."

Thus, before deciding what to do with an innovation, an established company must carefully assess whether the market created by the new way of competing is related to its existing market. This assessment of relatedness must go beyond cosmetic similarities. Simple as this might sound, it is often a truly thorny issue. Recent academic work on diversification has suggested that traditional measures of relatedness provide an incomplete and potentially exaggerated picture of the scope for a corporation to exploit interrelationships between two businesses.[1] This is because traditional measures look at relatedness only at the industry or market level, whereas the relatedness that matters is that between strategic assets. Appendix C describes the arguments against traditional measures of relatedness in more detail, and offers a methodology for measuring it correctly.

Looking at the issue of strategic relatedness from the perspective of an established competitor contemplating how to respond to a business-model innovation, the key question that needs to be asked is whether the new market created by the new business model is "strategically related" to the existing business. In other words, could I transfer strategic assets from my business to this new business, or are the two businesses only related in a superficial and cosmetic manner? The mistake that established competitors make is to assume that because the new market lies on the periphery of their industry, it would be easy for them to compete in it. This may be far from the real situation that they find should they enter the new market. Therefore, if the answer to the relatedness question is not an emphatic yes, the established firm may be better off ignoring the new business model.

Response Three: Disrupt the Disruptors

Another way for established companies to respond to an invading business model is to counterattack it—preferably in a manner similar to the way the innovators attacked them in the first place. Recall that the strategy that innovators employ is to develop a *second* value proposition, different from the value proposition that established companies compete on. They then attack by claiming to be good enough in the value proposition of the established competitors and superior in something else. What the established competitors could do is develop a *third* value proposition by emphasizing a different set of attributes from those promoted by the innovators. They can then attack their attackers by claiming, "We are good enough in the innovators' value proposition and superior in yet another dimension."

The way the Swiss watch industry responded to the Japanese attack in the late 1970s helps illustrate this point. As pointed out in Chapter Five, the Swiss used to dominate the global watch industry. They succeeded in doing so by selling their watches on the basis of Swiss craftsmanship and accuracy of the mechanical watch movement. This dominance all but evaporated in the 1970s when companies such as Seiko (from Japan) and Timex (from the United States) introduced a major innovation in the watch market—namely, cheap watches that used quartz technology and provided added functionality and features.

As with every business-model innovation, the innovators did not attack by trying to become better at the product attributes that the Swiss were emphasizing (that is, quality of the movement and accuracy of the watch). Instead, they focused on different performance attributes—price and functionality. At first, the new products attracted a totally different group of customers from the ones that valued what the Swiss were offering. It wasn't long, however, before even the customers who valued accuracy were attracted to the new watches. The Swiss share of global world production declined from 48 percent in 1965 to 15 percent by 1980.

The response of the established Swiss watch industry should be a lesson to all companies facing similar attacks in their business. Instead of adopting the new way of playing the game, the Swiss responded by introducing the Swatch. The new watch did not pretend to be better than Seiko or Timex in price or features (the performance attributes that the innovators at the time were emphasizing). Instead, the Swatch counterattacked by emphasizing different product attributes—style and variety. At the same time, by keeping the price of the Swatch low, the Swiss were able to successfully make the claim that the Swatch was good enough in price and superior in style and design. Thus, instead of responding to the invading game B by embracing it, they went after it by creating game C. Since its launch in 1983, Swatch has become the world's most popular timepiece, with more than 100 million sold around the world.

Two other companies that are currently responding in a manner similar to Swatch's response are Apple and British Airways. After its personal computer business came under attack from Dell and Compaq on the basis of price and technology, Apple responded by emphasizing style and design as the performance attributes of its products—witness the Apple iMac. Similarly, after its airline market was attacked by easyJet and Ryanair on the basis of price and point-to-point flying, British Airways responded by emphasizing comfort and luxury in its service offering—witness the introduction of seats that become flat beds and the luxurious executive lounges around the world.

The disrupt-the-disruptor strategy is a viable way of responding to an invading business model, but the key to success is to discover a genuine third value proposition to emphasize. This is not as easy as it sounds; the new value proposition must meet a number of criteria if it's going to be successful. Specifically:

- The new value proposition must be substantially different from what's on offer at the moment.
- It must be attractive to a big enough customer segment to make it economically viable to offer.
- It must be difficult for competitors to imitate, replicate, or substitute.

The strategy is also risky. The biggest mistake that companies make is to offer a third value proposition that nobody wants. This is classic overengineering of the product and it's easy to fall into. Another mistake that companies make is to keep adding benefits to their offering without investing enough to make it good enough in what the innovators are offering. Being superior in something is not enough. It's only when they can claim that they are good enough in what the innovators are offering *and* superior in something else that established firms can hope to succeed with this strategy.

Response Four: Embrace the New Business Model and Play Two Games

A fourth option available to established firms is to simply adopt the new business model. The decision whether to adopt it or not must be based on a detailed cost-benefit analysis, influenced by a number of factors specific to the firm. Once the decision is taken to adopt it, the question that arises is how? Even when an established company has resigned itself to the fact that the new business model is here to stay, finding a way to adopt it next to its existing business model could be problematic.

As discussed already, insufficient resources and limited managerial attention are only two of the costs facing these firms—and not even the major ones! What really creates problems for established firms is the fact that the new business model is conflicting with the established way of competing. In fact, given the existence of conflicts between the two business models, it is surprising that so many established firms consider adopting a second business model, let alone decide to go ahead. In my 2002 survey on how incumbents responded to invading business models, I specifically asked those firms that embraced the new business model to explain why they embarked on such a difficult and risky strategy. Figure 6.2 lists some of the reasons provided, along with the reactions of companies that decided not to try the new model.

As expected, managerial perceptions about the size and importance of the conflicts facing them varied considerably between companies that embraced the new business model and those that did not. Not surprisingly, those firms that viewed these potential conflicts as serious risks to their existing business decided not to embrace the new business model. The firms that actually did embrace the innovations regarded these conflicts as manageable. This finding is consistent with arguments in the strategic positioning literature that argue that the higher the degree of conflicts (or positioning trade-offs) between two strategic positions, the lower the likelihood that an established firm will embrace a new strategic position.

What was the major motivation behind the decision to embrace a second business model? My survey findings suggest that for the most part the established firms viewed the innovation as an opportunity to improve (not just defend) their existing competitive position in the industry and increase their market share.

Figure 6.2.   The Risks of Competing with Two Business Models at Once.

Please assess the difficulty of trying to compete in two different strategic positions at the same time based on the following risks:

By embracing the new business model, we *risk:*

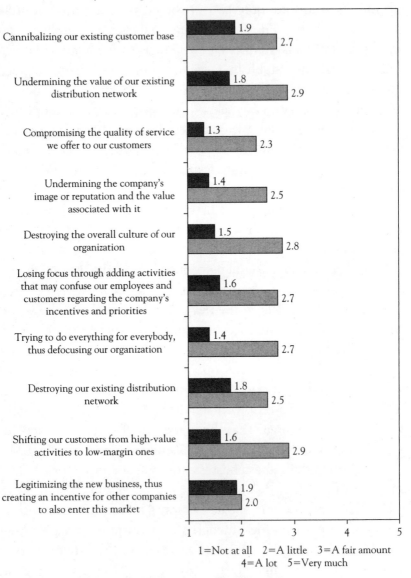

1=Not at all   2=A little   3=A fair amount
4=A lot   5=Very much

■ Companies that adopted the innovation
■ Companies that did not adopt the innovation

As shown in Figure 6.3, the established firms had a number of objectives in mind when they decided to embrace the innovation—and for the most part, they were successful in achieving these objectives.

Compared to the companies that did not embrace the new business model, those that did so felt that the new market would grow considerably in the future. To minimize friction with their established business, they developed products and services for the

Figure 6.3. Objectives of Firms That Adopted New Business Models and How Effective They Were in Achieving Them.

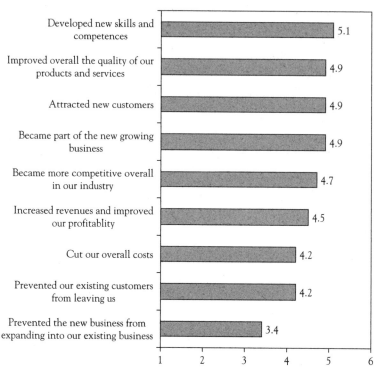

Please rate your effectiveness in responding to the emergence of the new business based on the following criteria:

Developed new skills and competences	5.1
Improved overall the quality of our products and services	4.9
Attracted new customers	4.9
Became part of the new growing business	4.9
Became more competitive overall in our industry	4.7
Increased revenues and improved our profitablity	4.5
Cut our overall costs	4.2
Prevented our existing customers from leaving us	4.2
Prevented the new business from expanding into our existing business	3.4

1=Very ineffective   2=Ineffective   3=Somewhat ineffective
4=Somewhat effective   5=Effective   6=Very effective

new market that were, on average, different from those in the established market in a number of dimensions (such as targeted customer segment, level of personal service provided, price, and overall characteristics). Many of them entered the new business through a separate unit, but many also chose to compete in the new business through their existing organizational structure and divisions. The challenges of competing with dual business models, either in a separate unit or within the existing organization, are discussed in Chapters Four and Five.

Response Five: Migrate to the New Business Model but Scale It Up

The fifth option available to established firms is to abandon their existing business model and embrace the new business model wholeheartedly. But in doing so, their goal should not be to simply imitate the innovation but to scale it up and grow it into a mass market. To appreciate how an established firm can do this, let's consider a few examples.

Consider the online bookselling innovation. Contrary to popular belief, the first online bookstore was started not by Amazon .com but by Charles Stack, an Ohio-based bookseller, in 1991. Stack got his Web site up and running in January 1993. Amazon, popularly recognized as the innovator in online bookselling, was actually third or fourth, opening its Web site fully two years after Stack, in February 1995. The two first movers in the business—Charles Stack and Computer Literacy Bookstore—were eventually acquired by Barnes & Noble.

Similarly, the first online brokers were two Chicago firms, Howe Barnes Investments and Security APL Inc., which launched a joint venture called Net Investor in January 1995 to offer Internet-based stock trading. Six years later, they were dwarfed by the success of Charles Schwab, which took over Internet brokerage and made it its own. A similar fate awaited CompuServe, which lost out to America Online in online services; Apple

Computer, which lost the PDA market to Palm; Atari, which created the video game market in 1972 and then lost it to Sony and Nintendo; and Osborne Computer, which produced the first portable computer and then lost out to Apple and IBM.

All these examples highlight one key point: innovation involves two essentially different activities—coming up with a new product or business-model idea, and creating a market out of that idea. For an innovation to be successful, these activities have to be coupled effectively—but *there is no need for the same firm to do both.* One firm may come up with the idea of a new and disruptive way of playing the game and another may take the idea and scale it up into a mass market.

In fact, the skills and competences needed for scaling up an idea are essentially different from the skills and competences needed to come up with the new idea. This gives the established firm a window of opportunity: allow small or entrepreneurial firms to come up with a new business-model idea and then move in and adopt the idea as their own. In the final analysis, this is the area where established firms have a competitive advantage over innovators: their skills and competences are better suited to stealing others' ideas and growing them into big markets. All this means that established firms can respond to a business-model innovation introduced by another firm by embracing the new way and growing it into a mass market.

To do this successfully, a firm needs to make serious investments in production so that it can produce a high-quality product very economically. It must also be able to help sway consumers and create the kind of consensus that would support the proposed dominant design. It needs to be able to identify and then reach out to the many potential consumers who are ready to purchase the new product or service but are unwilling to shoulder the risk of choosing between the many alternatives that first appear on the market. Creating an organization which can serve a large and rapidly growing market is also a requirement if the firm is to facilitate the growth of the market.

Established firms are typically slow movers, and they ought to be. Assembling this list of skills is a formidable undertaking. Most of the investments that are required involve substantial sunk costs, which should not be undertaken lightly. Further, what starts the bandwagon running toward a particular dominant design is the substantive presence of a major-league champion, and, indeed, the arrival of one or more players of this type in a market sends a clear signal to all concerned that the market is about to develop in new and very profitable ways. Only big-name established competitors can send such a credible signal.

In short, established competitors have the option of adopting somebody else's business-model innovation and growing it into a mass market. This idea is neither new nor novel. Other researchers such as Schnaars (1994) and Tellis and Golder (2002) have argued as much. What is amazing is how few of the established competitors who come under attack from business-model innovations even consider this option. In my own survey, many of the established companies that I interviewed talked about this option, but none of them chose to implement it. Yet history suggests that companies that pursue this option successfully create for themselves the basis for tremendous growth for years to come (for example, see Schnaars). Established companies must not be so quick in discarding this response option.

When to Do What

All in all, established companies can respond to business-model innovations in five different ways. But which of these responses is the right one for a specific firm?

Obviously, the answer to this question depends on a number of factors, such as the firm's position in its industry, its competences, the rate at which the new market is growing, the nature of the innovator who introduced the new business model, and so on. However, past research (for example, Chen and Hambrick, 1995; Chen and MacMillan, 1992; Chen and Miller, 1994;

Chen, Smith, and Grimm, 1992; Smith, Grimm, Chen, and Gannon, 1989) has identified two major factors that influence how companies should respond to major threats in their businesses: ability to respond and motivation to respond.

In the case of business-model innovation, the *ability* of an established firm to respond is determined by several factors, such as the firm's portfolio of skills, its wealth of resources, and the time it has at its disposal. But the most important factor that influences a firm's ability to respond is the nature and size of the conflicts that exist between the traditional business and the new business: the higher the conflicts, the lower the ability to respond. Similarly, the firm's *motivation* to respond is determined by factors such as the rate at which the innovation is growing and how threatening it is to the main business. But the major factor affecting motivation is how strategically related the new business is to the existing one: the more strategically related the new business is, the more motivated the firm will be to respond.

When the two factors are plotted on a matrix, the result is Figure 6.4—with the following implications: when the firm's motivation to respond is low (either because the innovation is not growing fast enough or is not threatening to the traditional business), the established firm should ignore it and focus on its own business (no matter what its ability to respond is). On the other hand, if the firm's motivation to respond is high, it should either attempt to destroy the innovation or embrace it wholeheartedly by abandoning its traditional business (when its ability to respond is low because of major conflicts), or imitate the innovation (when its ability to respond is high because conflicts are minor).

Needless to say, these recommendations are only applicable on average. Every firm would have to determine its own specific response according to the unique circumstances facing it. But appreciating that the new ways of competing are not inherently superior to the existing ways and that established firms have a number of options in responding to them (other than embracing them) is half the battle won.

Figure 6.4.   How to Respond to Business-Model Innovations: When to Do What.

	Low	High
High	Focus on your own business OR Ignore it (it is not your business)	Adopt and separate OR Adopt and keep inside OR Counterattack and destroy
Low	Focus on your own business	Counterattack (disrupt the disruptor) OR Embrace it and scale it up

Ability to Respond (vertical axis)

Motivation to Respond (horizontal axis: Low, High)

Summary

- Responding to a business-model innovation is not synonymous with imitating it. Various responses are possible, and adopting the innovation is only one of them.

- An established firm has five major ways to respond to the business-model innovation that invades its market:

   (a) Respond to the threat by investing in your business model to make it even more attractive than it is right now.

   (b) Ignore the new way of doing business because it is not really your business.

   (c) Respond by creating a new game—in other words, disrupt the disruptors.

(d) Adopt the new business model, a strategy that will force the firm to compete with dual business models simultaneously.

(e) Imitate the idea and then scale it up into a mass market.

- Which of these responses is the right one for a specific firm depends on a number of factors such as the firm's position in its industry, its competences, the rate at which the innovation is growing, the nature of the innovator who introduced the innovation, and so on.

- Appreciating that the new ways of competing are not inherently superior to the existing ways—and that established firms have a number of options in responding to them—are prerequisites to a successful response.

7

WHEN WOULD ESTABLISHED FIRMS DISCOVER NEW BUSINESS MODELS?

Unquestionably, the characteristics of business-model innovations are such that most established firms—especially the successful ones—find them less than attractive. There are, however, at least three instances that include all the necessary incentives for established firms to take the initiative in innovating in this manner:

- When the current business model is failing
- When the established firm is entering another established market, in effect attacking entrenched competitors in that market
- When the established firm is *scaling up* a new market that is in its early formative years

Migrating from a Failing Business Model

The first case is obvious enough—when the existing business model is failing and the firm is looking for a turnaround strategy, innovation is unavoidable. It is not necessary that the turnaround strategy be a game-changing business model as defined in this book—a firm does not have to discover a new business model that enlarges the market for it to succeed. But in its search for a new winning strategy, the firm may actually stumble upon a business model that turns out to be a game-changing innovation.

Consider, for example, the case of K-Mart. In May 1959, when Harry Cunningham became president of S.S. Kresge, the company (which was originally founded in 1897) was second only to Woolworth among variety store chains. It was, however, in serious financial trouble. Cunningham spent two years studying the discount industry (and especially Korvette) and then set about transforming Kresge from a variety chain with 803 stores into the largest discount store operation in the United States. In the process, he renamed the company K-Mart. The decision was a particularly difficult one because, as Cunningham explained, "Discounting at the time had a terrible odor. . . . If I had announced my intentions ahead of time, I never would have made president."[1] Yet the move into discounting rejuvenated the company, and by 1976 K-Mart was doing almost twice the sales volume of Woolworth and was only second behind Sears among general merchandise retailers.

Another case where an established firm's search for a new strategy to replace a failing one led to a game-changing business-model innovation was the introduction of low-cost, direct banking in Denmark by Lan & Spar Bank in the late 1980s. The bank, originally founded in 1880 by Danish trade unions, was in poor financial health and in need of turnaround when Peter Schou took over in 1988. From the very beginning, Schou set out to convert the small savings bank into a direct bank based on telephone, fax, and mail access. In the process, he introduced what amounted to "online banking" in Denmark at least six years before the growth of the Internet led to the emergence of this business model in the United States.

In the early stages of its transformation (1989–92), the bank offered two concepts to its customers: it continued to offer regular service through its branch network, but it also took the offensive with direct banking (using the telephone at first and then the Internet) at much lower prices. The customer decided whether to do all financial transactions at a branch (where a price premium was charged) or from home with the direct bank concept (at a price discount). In 1993, the two were merged into the direct bank concept. The customers could choose what distribution method suited them (branch, PC, phone, fax) and the price charged was the same everywhere and considerably lower than competitors. For example, Lan & Spar's interest spread was only 3 percent compared to an industry average of 10 percent.

Within three years, Lan & Spar emerged as the most profitable bank in Denmark and its market share more than quadrupled. This success continued throughout the 1990s—from 1991 until 1996, the bank was on average the most profitable bank in Denmark. By 1997, when the direct bank concept had evolved into the world's first online real-time PC bank with Internet banking also on offer, the bank had moved from No. 42 in Denmark to No. 10. All this growth and success came about without the benefit of a single acquisition.

Both the K-Mart and Lan & Spar examples highlight the first type of situation where established companies would have an incentive to innovate in their existing industry by introducing game-changing business models. Simply out of necessity, the established firm abandons a failing business model and migrates to a new one that might (just might) turn out to be a game-changing innovation. The next two instances highlight cases where the established firm develops new business models not out of necessity but as a way of entering new markets.

New Market Entry in Established Markets

Consider the following success stories:

- In the spring of 1902, Jim Penney opened his first dry goods store in Kemmerer, Wyoming, and began his attack on the big retail chains of the time (including such biggies as Sears and Woolworth, which date back to 1886 and 1879, respectively). By 1940, the J.C. Penney Company had grown to 1,586 stores and annual sales of $302 million.

- In January 1936, Lever Bros. (a subsidiary of Unilever) introduced a new vegetable shortening called Spry in the U.S. market. The new product went against

Procter & Gamble's established market leader, Crisco, which had been introduced in 1912. The impact of Spry was phenomenal: in a single year, it had already reached half the market share of Crisco.

- In the early 1960s, Canon (until then a camera manufacturer) entered the photocopier business—a field totally dominated by Xerox. By the early 1980s, having seen such formidable competitors as IBM and Kodak attack this same market without much success, Canon emerged as the market leader in unit sales.

- In 1972, Texas Instruments (until then a semiconductor chip supplier) entered the calculator business—a field already occupied by biggies such as Hewlett-Packard, Casio, Commodore, Sanyo, Toshiba, and Rockwell. Within five years, TI emerged as the market leader.

- In 1982, Gannett introduced *USA Today* into the crowded (1,700 dailies) newspaper field. By 1993, the new entry was a top-selling newspaper with an estimated daily readership of five million.

- In 1987, Howard Schultz bought Starbucks from the original owners. In the next five years, he transformed the company from a chain of 11 stores to some 280 stores. Sale revenues grew from $1.3 million in 1987 to $163.5 million in 1993.

- In the late 1980s, Yamaha tried to revitalize its declining piano business by developing the digital technology that allows customers to either record live performances by the pianists of their choice or buy such recordings on diskettes and then play the same composition on their pianos. Sales in Japan have been explosive.

These are certainly pleasing stories of success, but there is more to them than meets the eye. The common theme underpinning all these success stories is simple: *every company succeeded dramatically in attacking an established industry leader without the help of a radical technological innovation.* This is not easy. In fact, existing academic evidence shows that attacking an established leader usually ends up in failure—notwithstanding recent well-publicized cases of market leaders (such as IBM and GM) losing to new competitors. How did these companies succeed where most failed?

The common element in all the successful attacks is game-changing business-model innovation. Whenever a firm enters a new market, it is in effect attacking the established competitors in that market. These competitors were in that market before the attacker showed up—as a result, they enjoy first-mover advantages. Simply attacking them by trying to be *better* than they are will most likely lead to failure. The strategy that has been shown to increase the probability of success in such instances is the strategy of attacking them like a guerrilla, employing a different business model from theirs.

Canon's Assault on Xerox

Consider the case of Canon. Back in the 1960s, Xerox had a lock on the copier market by following a well-defined (and successful!) strategy. The main elements of this strategy were as follows: Xerox segmented the market by copier volume and consciously decided to promote high-speed copiers so as to tap the corporate reproduction market. This inevitably defined Xerox customers as the big corporations, which by itself determined the distribution method adopted by Xerox: direct sales force. At the same time, Xerox decided to lease rather than sell its machines, a strategic choice that had worked well for Xerox in its earlier battles with 3M. Xerox's strategy proved to be a winner—throughout the 1960s and early 1970s, Xerox maintained a return on equity (ROE) of around 20 percent.

This strategy proved so successful that several new competitors (such as IBM and Kodak) tried to enter this huge market by basically adopting the same or similar strategies. For example, IBM entered the market in 1970 with its first model, the IBM Copier I, which was clearly addressing the medium- and high-volume segments and was marketed by IBM's sales force on a rental basis. Similarly, Kodak entered the market in 1975 with the Ektaprint 100, which was aimed for the high-volume end of the market and was sold as a high quality–low price substitute to the Xerox machines.

Neither of these corporate giants managed to make substantial inroads in the copier business. While this failure has many possible reasons, their inability to create a distinctive position for themselves was undoubtedly one of them. Unlike Xerox, both IBM and Kodak failed to identify or create a distinctive strategic position in the industry. Instead, they tried to colonize Xerox's position and fought for market share by trying to become better than Xerox. Given the first-mover advantages that Xerox enjoyed in its own strategic position, it is no surprise that IBM and Kodak failed.

Canon, on the other hand, chose to play the game differently. Having determined in the early 1960s to diversify out of cameras and into copiers, Canon segmented the market by end user and decided to target small and medium-sized businesses while also producing copiers for the individual. At the same time, Canon decided to sell its machines through a dealer network rather than lease them, and while Xerox emphasized the speed of its machines, Canon elected to concentrate on quality and price as its differentiating features (see Table 7.1). Cutting the story short, where IBM's and Kodak's assault on the copier market failed, Canon's succeeded: within twenty years of attacking Xerox, Canon emerged as the market leader in volume terms.

Table 7.1. Xerox Versus Canon: A Case of Different Business Models.

Strategy Component	Xerox	Canon
Product	Plain paper copiers (PPCs)	Start with coated paper copiers and then move to PPCs
Copier volume	High	Low, then high
Targeted customers	Big corporations	End users
Method of selling	Lease	Sell
Distribution	Sales force	Dealer network
Differentiating features	Speed	Quality and price

Again, the success of Canon has many reasons. Notice, however, that just as Xerox did twenty years earlier, Canon created for itself *a distinctive strategic position* in the industry—a position that was different from Xerox's position. Whereas Xerox targeted big corporations as its customers, Canon went after small companies and individuals; while Xerox emphasized the speed of its machines, Canon focused on quality and price; and whereas Xerox used a direct sales force to lease its machines, Canon used its dealer network to sell its copiers. Rather than try to beat Xerox at its own game, Canon triumphed by creating its own unique strategic position.

As in the case of Xerox, these were not the only choices available to Canon, and undoubtedly serious debates and disagreements must have taken place within Canon as to whether these were the right choices to pursue. Yet choices were made, and a clear strategy with sharp and well-defined boundaries was put in place. As in the case of Xerox, Canon was successful because it chose a unique and well-defined strategic position in the industry—one with distinctive customers, products, and activities.

Apple's Attack on IBM

Another classic example of a company that succeeded in entering a new market through a game-changing business model innovation is Apple Computer. Back in the mid-1970s, the established market leader in the computer business was IBM. These were the main elements of the successful IBM strategy:

- Target corporations as customers
- Manufacture the heart of the computer—the microprocessor
- Write the software for the computers
- Sell the computers through a direct sales force

Apple came along and totally changed these norms: it targeted individuals and small businesses as its customers, purchased its microprocessors from an outside source, and started distributing its machines through retail stores across the country.

Several other companies also succeeded against the odds in entering new markets (and attacking established competitors who enjoyed first-mover advantages): Dell did it in the PC business by bypassing the intermediaries and selling directly to the end consumer; Nucor Steel attacked the big integrated steel manufacturers by using minimills—a completely different process for fabricating steel; Medco Containment Services strategically innovated by providing companies with prescription drugs through the mail rather than through retail drugstores; Southwest Airlines entered the crowded airline industry by flying point to point rather than using the hub-and-spoke system.

All these examples highlight my main point: it is difficult but feasible to successfully attack the established industry leaders or to successfully enter a new market where established players exist. The strategy that seems to improve the probability of success in these situations involves breaking the rules. The implication of this is simple: any established company that aims to enter another market where entrenched competitors exist must consider doing so only through business-model innovation. Attacking a crowded new market represents the first instance when the incentives are right for established firms to proactively seek to discover new business models. But there is another instance when established firms will have the right incentives to do so.

Scaling Up New Markets

The necessary incentives to develop game-changing business models are also in place when established firms attempt to scale up a newly created, emerging market. To appreciate this, recall from Chapter Six the key point that discovering and scaling up a new market are essentially different activities that *do not necessarily have to be performed by the same firm*. In fact, in the majority of cases, the companies that pioneer radical innovations are not the ones that ultimately scale them up.[2]

Consider, for example, the following cases:

Online Services

CompuServe created this market in 1979 with the provision of its first online service, the CompuServe information service. Over time, CompuServe used its pioneering efforts in videotex technology to enable users to not only access information but also perform banking and shopping transactions from their homes. Additional services such as e-mail, electronic bulletin boards, and forums were added throughout the 1980s as new competitors (such as AOL and Prodigy) entered the market. By 1990, the market for online services had about one million subscribers and CompuServe was its clear leader. Then the market simply exploded: while it took more than ten years for the market to grow to its first million subscribers, it took only another seven for the market to increase ten times, to more than ten million subscribers by the start of 1998. By then, AOL had emerged as the clear leader, having acquired CompuServe's subscriber base and content operations in February 1998.

Personal Digital Assistants

Apple created the market for personal digital assistants (PDAs) when it announced its plans to introduce the Apple Newton in May 1992 (and eventually introduced it in August 1993). The Newton was using handwriting-recognition software developed by Apple and was small enough to fit in one's hand. John Sculley (Apple's CEO) called it "nothing less than a revolution" and predicted that it would launch "the mother of all markets," with PDAs constituting a trillion-dollar market. A few months later, Palm released the Palm Zoomer. Both products fared poorly in the market, but this did not stop competitors (such as HP, Psion, Casio, and Microsoft) from rushing in with offerings of their own. In April 1995, Palm (then a division of US Robotics) introduced the Pilot organizer, which not only used the Graffiti interface software but was also the first organizer to connect to a PC (allowing the synchronization of information between the two machines). The market for PDAs took off—from a few hundred thousand units sold in 1995 to millions of units in two years. In the year 2000 alone, more than 6.5 million PDAs were sold, and Palm emerged as the undisputed leader with 70 percent market share.

Both these examples highlight a simple idea—something that the famous economist Joseph Schumpeter pointed out a hundred years ago: successful innovation is essentially a coupling process that requires the linking of two distinct activities—the discovery of a new product or service and its initial testing in the market, which, if successful, creates a new *market niche* (what Apple and CompuServe did in their respective markets), and the transformation of the innovation from a little niche into a *mass market* (what Palm and AOL did).

Both activities are, obviously, important and necessary for successful innovation—but, as the examples above show, *there is no need for the same firm to do both.* Apple and CompuServe came up with the product ideas but Palm and AOL created the mass markets for these products. In fact, the firm that comes up with a new idea—the pioneer—is rarely the one that creates a mass market out of that idea. Everybody derides Xerox for coming up with zillions of new products and technologies at its PARC research center and then failing to bring them to market. The truth of the matter is that this happens more often than people think!

Who Scales Up New Markets?

Usually, the firms that scale up new markets are the big, established firms. They are the ones that have the necessary skills and assets to grow a niche market into a mass market. More important, the way that established companies scale up new markets is through game-changing business-model innovation in the manner described in this book. Specifically, they succeed by developing a business model that is substantially different from the one used by the early firms in a market.

The early pioneers that rush to colonize a new market do so by emphasizing the *technical attributes* of the product. Most of the time, this happens simply because the entrepreneurs who created the company are engineers. It is their technical and engineering skills that allowed them to translate a certain technology into a product, and it is the functionality of this product that attracts the early consumers.

You see this emphasis on the technical attributes of the product in the early phases of all young markets. For example, Xerox sold its copiers by emphasizing their functionality and speed of copying; Ampex sold its VCRs on the quality of their recording; Leica sold its cameras on the quality of their lenses, which guaranteed quality pictures; Cuisinart sold its food processors by focusing on its engineering skills, which translated into high-quality kitchen equipment; and Apple sold its handheld computer on its breakthrough handwriting-recognition software.

This emphasis on the technical aspects and functionality of the product early on in the evolution of a new market is understandable. To begin with, the product comes into being because it satisfies a certain customer need. Unless the product has the necessary technical features to meet this need, it will not succeed. Second, the entrepreneurs who created the product are engineers—they are the ones who understand the technology and toil for years to translate it into a workable product that can satisfy an unmet customer need. Their natural inclination is to emphasize the things they know and the things they believe make their product better than other products. Third, at the start of any new market, the performance of early products is still below what most customers expect or want. This means that a competitor that invests in improving the performance of its product, bringing its level closer to what customers want, will benefit from such investment. This implies that competition in the early stages of the market is based on product features and performance—early pioneers compete against each other by adding functionality to their products.

The efforts of these pioneers create the first market niche. The consumers that rush to purchase the new product tend to be technology enthusiasts or early adopters. They don't particularly mind that the product is flawed or expensive—they just want to get their hands on the newest toy in the market. Obviously, these early adopters represent only a small fraction of the population. Therefore, by definition, the pioneers are targeting a niche market.

It is at this stage that consolidators move in and steal the market away. What they do is shift the basis of competition from

Table 7.2. Scaling Up a Market by Emphasizing Different Product Attributes.

Industry	Pioneers	Product Attributes Emphasized by Pioneers	Firms Scaling Up the Market	Product Attributes Emphasized by the Scaling-Up Firms
Photocopying	(Haloid) Xerox and 3M	Speed and quality of copying	Canon	Price, size, quality
Handheld computers	Apple (Newton)	Handwriting-recognition software, features	Palm (3Com)	Price, size, and pc synchronization
Online brokerage	K. Aufhauser, Security APL, and Howe Barnes	Convenience	Charles Schwab	Price, convenience, speed of execution
Portable computers	Osborne and Apple	Technology, features	IBM	Price, size
Video recorders	Ampex	High-quality recording	JVC and Sony	Price, size, weight
Online bookselling	Books.com, Charles Stack, and clbooks.com	Convenience	Amazon.com	Availability, convenience, price
Motorcycles	Triumph and Harley Davidson	Speed and power	Honda	Size and price

(Continued)

Table 7.2. (continued)

Industry	Pioneers	Product Attributes Emphasized by Pioneers	Firms Scaling Up the Market	Product Attributes Emphasized by the Scaling-Up Firms
35mm cameras	Leica	Quality (of lenses and pictures), engineering	Canon and Nikon	Price, ease of use
Microwave ovens	Tappan Stove Co., Raytheon, and Litton	Speed and quality	Panasonic, Sharp, and Samsung	Price
Internet service provider	CompuServe	Technology, info content, speed, and features	America Online	Ease of use, price
Food processors	Cuisinart	Speed, features, quality	Black & Decker	Price
Shaving razors	Cutthroat razors and Autostrop Safety Razor Co.	High-grade steel for lifetime of sharpening	Gillette	Disposable blade, price, ease of use
Pocket calculators	Bowmar	Speed, features, ease of use	Texas Instruments	Price
Disposable diapers	Chicopee Mills (Johnson & Johnson)	Ease of use, quality	Procter & Gamble	Price, ease of use
Fax machines	Xerox	Quality and speed	Sharp	Price, ease of use

technical performance to other product attributes such as *price and quality*. They do this by cutting the price of the product to a mass-market level while at the same time improving the quality of the product to make it acceptable to the average consumer. All of a sudden, the product becomes attractive to the mass market and rapid growth follows.[3] Table 7.2 shows that the tactic of shifting the emphasis from the technical attributes of the product to price and quality is something that consolidators have used in industry after industry. The evolution of the disposable diaper market in the United States illustrates this point well.

The Procter & Gamble Pampers Example

Most people think that Procter & Gamble (P&G) pioneered the disposable diaper market by introducing Pampers in 1961. The truth is that although P&G was the first to popularize the disposable diaper to the mass market, credit for pioneering the first disposable diaper must go to Chicopee Mills, a unit of Johnson & Johnson. Chicopee Mills introduced the first disposable diaper—Chux—as early as 1932. Two other providers, Sears and Montgomery Ward, also launched disposable diapers before P&G did. However, these products did not prove long-term successes and failed to capture the public imagination.

By 1956, disposable diapers accounted for only 1 percent of diaper changes in the United States. The main reason was their high cost (about 9 cents per unit), which was more than double what laundry service cost (and much more costly than home washing). Another reason was the product's performance: not only did the diapers come with no attachment tapes, meaning they had to be anchored with traditional safety pins, but even worse, their absorbent core was made of several layers of tissue paper, which led to a high leakage rate. Thus, consumers treated disposable diapers as a luxury item to be used only on special occasions (such as traveling with babies).

Pampers was introduced by P&G in 1961. It owes its existence to Victor Mills, a chemical engineer working for the company. In 1956, Procter & Gamble acquired a paper pulp plant, and Mills's team of engineers was given the job of figuring out what to do with it. A grandfather by then, Mills was reminded of how much he hated changing diapers, and it occurred to him that using cellulose fibers instead of paper would vastly improve the performance of a diaper. The challenge, however, was how to apply this idea to the design of an acceptable disposable diaper for the mass market at a reasonable price. On the design front, the diaper had to be soft enough to be comfortable, yet strong enough not to disintegrate when wet. On the price front, the firm needed an efficient manufacturing process that would allow it to manufacture the diaper at such a low cost as to make its price attractive for the average consumer.

It took five years of research before the first Pampers was finally launched in 1961. The initial test market was not successful: even though the product was rated highly by consumers, it was still too expensive for most of them. It took another five years of research and improvements in manufacturing technology before P&G was able to produce the product at a low enough unit price to stimulate a mass market. Drawing upon its vast experience in grocery marketing and its early research efforts, the company had set as a target a retail price of 6.2 cents per diaper. This meant it had to reduce manufacturing costs to around 3 cents, something that entailed significant reductions in raw material costs and a more efficient manufacturing process.

It was only when P&G succeeded in producing high-quality diapers at a cost of 3.5 cents a unit that Pampers was finally given a national rollout in 1966 (at the retail price of 5.5 cents per diaper). At such a low price, Pampers became an instant success.

The U.S. disposable diaper market grew from $10 million in 1966 to $370 million by 1973, and demand for the product was so high that the firm struggled to satisfy it. The success of Pampers was so overwhelming that the pioneer of this market—Johnson & Johnson—withdrew its brand (Chux) from the market and focused on private labeling, leaving P&G in control of the branded market by 1981.

This example shows how a late entrant scaled up and captured the market by cutting the price of the product while still improving its quality. But often, a late entrant captures the market even with a product which is inferior in quality to the product of the pioneers! It is instructive to understand why that happens.

As argued earlier, the efforts of the pioneers create the first market niche. Unfortunately for them, two things follow that set the stage for their downfall. First, as a result of their investments in improving the performance of the product, it can actually reach performance levels that surpass customer needs. At that stage, any additional investments to improve the performance of the product further are not really necessary. But the pioneers cannot help it! Their engineering cultures go to work, and sure enough, more and more money goes into R&D to improve the product further and add to its functionality. All this happens even though they know full well that the customers do not need nor will they ever use the added functionality.

Overengineering of the product is linked to the second change taking place: the extra investments and incremental additions to the product's performance do not come free. Rising costs lead to rising prices. The high price, in turn, limits the attraction of the product; it appeals only to the small market segment made up of technology enthusiasts and early adopters.

The combination of these two factors is what gives consolidators their chance to move in and steal the market away. They know that all they have to do is to produce a product that is good enough in performance but cheaper than what is on the market now. Their product may not be as good as the product of the pioneers, but this does not really matter. The early adopters are not attracted to these obviously inferior products—*but the average mass-market consumer is!* To the latter and much larger group, this is a product that is acceptable in quality *and* cheap. Over time, the consolidators may improve the performance of their products to such an extent that even technically astute customers (the early adopters) begin to find them attractive (and so switch). But this is not absolutely necessary. As long as they control the mass market, the consolidators are happy to leave a few little niches for other competitors to feed on. Their overriding objective is to make a product that is not necessarily the best—just one that is good enough in performance and superior in price.

The Palm Example

The story of how Palm conquered the handheld computer market illustrates this point well. Apple Computer created the market by introducing the Apple Newton in August 1993. Palm followed in October with the introduction of the Palm Zoomer. Both products flopped—not only did they have poor handwriting-recognition software but they were also expensive, heavy, and overburdened with PC functions (like spreadsheet software and printing functions) that made them slow.

By the mid-1990s, Palm was really at a dead end. It was then that it got acquired by US Robotics—a much bigger firm with financial and marketing clout. The following year, the Palm Pilot was introduced, and it proved to be a hit with the consumers. The infusion of resources, established distribution outlets, and branding expertise from the bigger parent certainly helped

Palm scale up the PDA market. But what's of interest here is the nature of the product that allowed Palm to achieve such a feat.

Comparing the Apple Newton with the Palm Pilot, it is safe to suggest that the Newton was a much more sophisticated product in technical terms. And that's exactly the point! The Newton was like a scaled-down PC, loaded with all kinds of software. By contrast, the Pilot was conceived as an accessory to the PC, to be used primarily as an organizer with connectivity to the PC. It was also simple and fast and, more important, cheap ($299). The Pilot was a huge triumph, despite being less sophisticated than the Newton. It was less sophisticated than the Newton but was exactly what the mass market wanted and needed!

By the turn of the century, Palm controlled more than 70 percent of the market. In the years that followed the Pilot's introduction, Microsoft developed its own operating system for handheld computers—the Windows CE—and hardware vendors such as HP, Casio, and Philips entered the handheld market carrying this operating system. Repeated attempts by Microsoft to make inroads in this market by adding more features and more memory have failed. Microsoft's motto of "more is better" has come up against Palm's "smaller, faster, cheaper" and at least in the early stages of this battle, Palm was winning. Sure, the Palm has recently fallen prey to the BlackBerry (introduced by Research in Motion), but the possible demise of Palm should not take away from the fact that it was its game-changing business model that enabled the handheld computer niche to grow into a mass market.

Both the Palm and the P&G examples highlight a simple point: to scale up a newly created market from a little niche into a big mass market, one needs to adopt a business model fundamentally different from the one that pioneers have used. Specifically, consolidators need to emphasize different product attributes, target different customers, and sell and distribute the product in different ways from those of the pioneers. The scaling up of a newly created niche market represents a second instance where established companies have the necessary incentives to proactively engage in game-changing business-model innovation.

Summary

- The majority of business-model innovations are introduced by newcomers to an industry (rather than established competitors).

- Newcomers predominate because business-model innovations display certain characteristics that make them unattractive to established firms. A firm that already operates one business model will have few incentives to introduce another business model in its industry.

- There are, however, three instances when established firms would have the incentives to pioneer a new business model:

  When the current business model is failing

  When the established firm is entering another established market, in effect attacking entrenched competitors in that market

  When the established firm is *scaling up* a new market that is in its early formative years

8

RETHINKING INNOVATION
IN THE BIG FIRM

I want to finish with a key point that I started this book with: innovation is not one thing. There are different types of innovation, all capable of creating new market space. Furthermore, what a company needs to do to achieve one type of innovation may be totally different from what it must do to achieve another type.

At the very minimum, innovations sort neatly into two groups. The first group consists of innovations (such as product extensions or the creation of new brands) that tend to build on a firm's existing skills, competences, mind-sets, and culture. They are neither competence-destroying nor complementary asset–destroying—instead, they are what Christensen (1997) labeled *sustaining innovations*. The second group consists of innovations (such as the creation of radical new products or business-model innovations) that tend to undermine the firm's existing skills, competences, and values. They are both competence-destroying and complementary asset–destroying—what Christensen labeled *disruptive innovations*.

To achieve the first type of innovation, a firm simply has to improve its existing "organizational environment." By *organizational environment*, I mean four basic elements:

- *The culture of the company*, which includes its norms, values, and unquestioned assumptions
- *The structure of the company*, comprising not only its formal hierarchy but also its physical setup as well as its systems (information, recruitment, market research, and the like)

- *The incentives in the company,* both monetary and nonmonetary
- *The people of the company,* including their skills and attributes

It is the combination of these four elements that creates the organizational environment, which in turn supports and promotes the firm's strategy of innovation.

Consider, for example, 3M, recognized worldwide as one of the most innovative companies in the world. How has 3M maintained its high level of innovation, year after year? How has its strategy of innovation been supported and promoted? A look at Figure 8.1 suggests that the answer to this question is "by expressly designing an organizational environment that promotes innovation." The culture, structure, incentives, and people at 3M have been explicitly designed and arranged to promote innovation.

What 3M has done is only a small fraction of what a company could do to promote the first type of innovation. Over the past fifty years, academics and consultants have developed a wealth of ideas on how a company could improve its existing organizational environment to promote this type of innovation—the next box provides a (long) laundry list of ideas. But try as its people may, *improving* the *existing* organizational environment of a firm will *not* produce the *second type* of innovation in the *firm's own industry.* Sure, as I explained in Chapter Seven, established firms have all the incentives to promote game-changing business-model innovation when they attempt to enter another industry or when they try to scale up another niche market. But when it comes to promoting business-model innovation in their own industries, this might be a bridge too far. To achieve this type of innovation, a firm needs to do much more than simply improve what it already has in its organizational environment.

Figure 8.1. Innovation at 3M.

Culture

- 3M policy allows employees to spend 15 percent of their time developing projects of their own choosing.
- Employees are encouraged to take the initiative and are empowered to make decisions. Failure is accepted.
- The pervading culture is characterized by the rule that you have to kiss a lot of frogs to find one prince.
- A flat hierarchy makes people feel responsible for everything that goes on in their divisions.

People

- By virtue of its incentives and culture, 3M attracts top scientists and engineers.
- The company is able to recruit and retain creative people with an entrepreneurial mind-set.
- Because of its dual career ladder, top scientists can coexist with top managers without internal competition.

Innovation

Structure

- 3M assigns cross-functional teams to work on research projects.
- Each team is headed by a "product champion" who is responsible for building culture.
- One of 3M's top managers becomes a "management sponsor" who helps the team secure resources and overcome bureaucratic obstacles.
- Divisions within 3M are run as separate companies. Divisional VPs have the same responsibility as a CEO in many other companies.
- Hierarchies within divisions are kept flat.
- The Annual Technology Fair allows scientists to showcase their latest research findings and exchange ideas and information.

Incentives

- The company has established career ladders for scientists that are separate from those for managers.
- Teams that introduce successful new products are rewarded.
- Successful new products can be spun off as separate divisions with their own profit-and-loss statements. The original product champion becomes divisional president.
- 3M has set a formal goal that 25 percent of sales must come from new products. Managerial performance is measured and rewarded according to this goal.

How to Promote Innovation

- Encourage participation from everybody and from every level in the hierarchy.
- Encourage experimentation and do not punish failures.
- Reward good ideas.
- Remove bureaucracy and encourage the flow of ideas and people across the firm.
- Develop a supportive culture.
- Promote innovators to signal the importance of innovation.
- Systematically analyze opportunities on an ongoing basis.
- Improve communications across departments and encourage "diagonal" rather than vertical and horizontal communications.
- Remember that effective innovations start small, are clearly focused, and try to do one specific thing.
- Keep things simple—overly complicated or clever innovations are usually unsuccessful because they are difficult to adapt or change as more about them or the market is learned.
- Make sure the number of projects is within the range the company can digest. Too much innovative activity at one time dilutes the effectiveness of the efforts.
- Concentrate on what you can do right now. Attempts as innovation "for the future" generally fail.
- Focus innovative efforts on your strengths, or be prepared to build new strengths. Innovations that stray from the core become diffuse and remain ideas.
- Generate an innovation-promoting corporate vision.
- Establish clear and cohesive goals, objectives, and strategies.
- Make sure top management and middle management agree on the desirability of the vision and objectives of an entrepreneurial strategy. In other words, make sure the strategy is supported from the top down.

- Encourage management of the process of innovation, not the project.
- Identify the ways in which corporate structure impedes innovation and correct them.
- Identify the individual markets or product and service areas where there is a need for an entrepreneurial strategy.
- Encourage planning and innovative activities at the lowest possible organizational levels.
- Provide timely, relevant feedback on achievement toward goals.
- Identify, confront, and accept the risk and uncertainty of a new venture.
- Involve employees in productivity improvement efforts.
- Tolerate and support specific types of failure.
- Learn from your mistakes.
- Make your strategy process democratic.
- Bring the characteristics of capitalism inside the organization.
- Create cross-functional teams.
- Create flat structures.
- Encourage attention to the outside marketplace and competition.
- Develop supportive compensation systems.
- Reward and recognize exceptional performance.
- Develop rewards proportionate to the risk being asked.
- Encourage long-term views.
- Encourage the perception of change as *opportunity* rather than change as *threat*.
- Maintain a limited number of new ventures at various start-up stages at one time.
- Encourage entrepreneurial efforts by making frequent and public statements in support of it.
- Develop special, separate funds and spending authority over them for use by those with a proven record of innovative success.

- Create small profit centers and provide separate budgets for new ventures.
- Organize new ventures as separate entities, and keep them away from established divisional management, allowing them to be responsive and quickly adaptive.
- Develop procedures to evaluate, screen, and develop new ideas and encourage middle management to keep the process moving.
- Keep venture groups small to take advantage of the small-company atmosphere that will develop.
- Provide freedom and funding in a controlled way, avoiding the main hazard of too much, too soon, with too little control—followed by too little, too late, with too much control.
- Develop procedures that systematically encourage employees to take risks.
- Make sure that the entrepreneur with the vision, the person or group responsible for development of the new idea, remains attached to and responsible for the new idea until it is launched and is either a success or a failure.
- Duplicate the climate of a small, independent, fast-growing company in as many ways as possible.

Conflicting Skills and Attitudes

Imagine the following scenario: You wake up one morning and decide that you don't like the way your seventy-year-old parents look. Nor do you think they live an active enough life. You decide that what they really need is a change—instead of golf, they should take up squash; instead of looking like seventy-year-olds, they should adopt a dietary and fitness regime designed to make them look young again; and instead of spending their time watching TV, they should visit the gym twice a day. You are so determined to achieve this transformation that you invest most of your free time, urging your parents along and giving them advice on what to do and when. In your quest to make them teenagers again, you know no boundaries!

How silly does this sound? Yet this is exactly what academics and other advisers have been trying to do with big, established companies. Not satisfied with how innovative they are, we have come up with all these "valuable" ideas and advice to make them more entrepreneurial so that they too—like all those agile and pioneering start-up firms—can create new markets and lay the foundations for the industries of the future. How? By developing the cultures and structures of the younger start-up firms. Look, we tell them. Don't you want to be like Dell or Cisco or Virgin? All you have to do is adopt *their* structures, cultures, and processes. Who says elephants can't dance? Just go on a diet and lose some of that excess weight, learn a few tricks from the younger firms, and off you go!

Unfortunately, the probability that such a thing will happen is equal to the probability that you will convert your parents into teenagers again. Zero.

The problem is not that established firms do not agree with these ideas or that they do not want to adopt them. To the contrary, they will find these recommendations (such as developing cultures that encourage experimentation or making their strategy process democratic or even developing a self-cannibalizing attitude) constructive and useful. But despite agreeing with all of this, they will not succeed in adopting these attitudes and cultures.

This is because they already have a set of skills and attitudes that they need to compete successfully in their existing businesses. This set of skills and attitudes makes them good at *exploitation*, which is exactly what they need to do well in their mature businesses. Now, all of a sudden, the so-called experts want them to also adopt a set of skills and attitudes that will make them good explorers. But the skills and attitudes needed for exploration are difficult to maintain alongside the skills and attitudes needed for exploitation—they often conflict with each other and rarely coexist smoothly. Attempting to bring on board the skills of exploration will most likely create a reaction from the organization. The organization's antibodies will go to work, and the new skills and attitudes will be rejected as unwanted foreign organs.

The point I am making here is not new. More than forty years ago, Burns and Stalker argued in *The Management of Innovation* that "organic" organizational forms cannot easily coexist with "mechanistic" organizations. And just three years ago, Silicon Valley entrepreneur Randy Komisar—famous for helping launch WebTV and TiVo among other companies—said:[1]

> Most large companies succeed and prosper because they have established policies and procedures designed around managing complex and large-scale operations. It's a very important skill, and a critical competitive advantage. But the psychology of creating and managing that sort of operation is 180 degrees off from the psychology of taking risks around launching new ideas. And [anyone with] the notion of being an intrapreneur—somebody who goes into a large organization to be at the vanguard of redirecting or cannibalizing the current business . . . will find that the process and procedures that make the mother ship so successful will do them in. The two approaches are at odds.

What I have been arguing in this book is a slight variant of this point. New business models are not only different from the business models that established firms already use in their main markets but (what is more important) in conflict with them. This means that it's not enough to proclaim the virtues of business-model innovation and expect established firms to just do it. They won't. Just like your elderly parents know the virtues of daily exercise but still do not do it, so do established firms know the advantages of developing new markets through business-model innovation but still won't do it. Discovering new business models is not the issue; the issue is organizational.

What to Do with Business-Model Innovation

It is for these (organizational) reasons that several academics have proposed that the way for established companies to promote this kind of innovation is through separate units. Resorting to a separate organizational entity is certainly a viable option and it is one that several companies have used successfully. For example, IBM chose to set up its PC organization in Boca Raton, Florida, away from the established IBM organization and away from corporate interference. However, as I pointed out in Chapter Four, this solution has a major drawback: by keeping the two businesses separate, the organization fails to exploit synergies between them. Not only could the new business benefit from the resources and knowledge of the established business, the established business itself could benefit from the vitality and experience of the new one.

Another option for established firms is to accept that the challenge of promoting competence-destroying innovations like business-model innovation is simply too formidable for them. Rather than attempt to do so themselves, they should subcontract the development of new business models to the horde of small start-up firms around the world that have the requisite skills and attitudes to succeed at this game. Established firms should, instead, concentrate on what they are good at—which is to move in after a small firm has proven the viability of a new business model and consolidate it into a mass market. After all, big firms have established one thing in their history: they are good at consolidating new markets. And being a consolidator has given them access to first-mover advantages—advantages that the vast majority of pioneers never got close to realizing.

This is a solution that I proposed in another book for another type of innovation that is as competence-destroying as business-model innovation: radical product innovation.[2] Practically speaking, what this means is that instead of spending valuable resources and managerial talent on developing new business models, established companies should aim to create, sustain, and nurture a network of feeder firms—of young, entrepreneurial firms that are busy experimenting with new business models. When the viability of the new business model has been proven or when the market created by the new business model has grown enough, the established firm could move in and build a new mass-market business on the platform that these feeder firms have provided, in the manner described in Chapter Six.

What I am proposing here is for the modern corporation to subcontract the creation of new business models to the market and for start-up firms to subcontract the consolidation of these new ways of competing to big established firms. This might strike some people as too radical an idea, but it is in fact a model that is widely accepted in industries where companies live and die on their ability to *continuously* bring creative new products to the market: creative industries such as movies, theaters, art galleries, and book or music publishing.[3]

Think about it. A major book publisher does not even try to create any of its "new products" (that is, the books) internally. It could, of course, attempt to do exactly that! That would involve hiring thousands of employees, giving each an office and a computer, and asking them to produce new books in return for a fixed salary (and a generous pension). But how silly does that sound? Surely, an organizational structure like that would be the fastest way to destroy creativity and innovation! And yet, that's exactly how the modern corporation is structured. Is it any surprise, then, that the modern corporation is not particularly known for its creativity and innovativeness?

Instead of attempting to do everything internally, a major book publisher goes out in the market, identifies potential product creators (that is, the authors), and signs them up to deliver their product to it. Once the product is created (outside the bureaucracy of the big firm), the author subcontracts the marketing, promotion, and distribution of the creation to the book publisher. Just as it would be silly for the big publisher to attempt to create the new products internally, it would be a similar act of folly for an individual author to attempt to sell and promote a book on a do-it-yourself basis. This division of labor builds on the strengths of each actor and is a solution that maximizes the welfare of everyone involved. Sure, there may be disagreements and problems between publisher and authors, but that's what management (or agents) are there for.

This arrangement appears to be the norm in several other creative industries. Therefore, to repeat my thesis: creative industries display a clear separation between those that create the product and those that promote, distribute, and sell it. Needless to say, the promoters must be knowledgeable about the latest technology and products so that they can make an intelligent assessment of whether a painting or a book or a recording is good enough for them to promote. But they do not have to be actively involved in its creation. If this organization of work functions well in creative industries, isn't it at least worth an attempt to import it into other industries that aspire to become more creative? I would be surprised if the organizational structure that characterizes creative industries cannot be readily imported into any industry that aspires to create new radical markets through business-model innovation.

Appendix A

EXAMPLES OF A FEW LESS WELL-KNOWN BUSINESS-MODEL INNOVATORS

Whenever academics talk about business-model innovators who succeeded by breaking the rules in their industries, the usual suspects are mentioned: The Body Shop, IKEA, Southwest, Swatch, CNN, Home Depot, Nucor, Dell, Starbucks, Bloomberg, and so on. But these frequently mentioned cases are far from the only business-model innovators to have found success in the market. Here, I provide a list of twenty less well-known business-model innovators.

1. Company: Kingfisher Airlines (Industry: Airline)

   Kingfisher Airlines is based in India. It is a major Indian luxury airline operating an extensive network to more than thirty destinations, with plans for regional and long-haul international services. Like Virgin Atlantic Airways, it redefined the travel experience for business and first-class travelers. For example, the Kingfisher Airlines Roving Agent makes sure that as soon as any of the company's guests start walking toward the security gate, an agent armed with a handheld device and printer confirms and prints out a boarding pass for them, saving their time.

2. Company: Priceline (Industry: Travel agent and other services)

   Priceline empowered consumers to "name their own price" for airline tickets and hotel rooms, then shopped these offers to marketers. Priceline's founder Jay Walker described the resulting transactions as a new ecosystem, which helped consumers realize lower prices while allowing marketers to turn excess inventory into profit and, in so doing, price-discriminate without damaging their brands or their published prices. Airline tickets and hotel reservations were only the starting point for Priceline, however.

Priceline.com also experimented with selling gasoline and groceries under the *Name Your Own Price* model in 2000, at the height of the dot-com bubble, through a partially owned affiliate, WebHouse Club. Priceline also got into the online auction business with *Priceline Yard Sales*, where individuals could use the Priceline system to haggle over various secondhand items and trade them in person. Priceline also sold long-distance telephone service and automobiles under the *Name Your Own Price* model. All these experiments were terminated in 2002. Another experiment, the *Name Your Own Rate* system for home loans, continues under a license with EverBank.

3. Company: Red Bull (Industry: Energy drinks)

Red Bull was initially developed in Thailand in 1987 and marketed to young people as an energy booster, using sassy advertising spots and the catchphrase "Red Bull gives you wings." In some countries, Red Bull commanded an 80 percent market share. In the United States, Red Bull enjoyed a 47 percent share of the energy drink market. A key element of Red Bull's marketing strategy has been to open up a market by securing unusual distribution. Red Bull relies heavily on bars and nightclubs for its sampling events. It also uses alternative sports to promote its product. It buys traditional advertising last. The image of Red Bull has luxury lifestyle identification. With only locally tailored marketing, Red Bull had seen its sales grow quickly. The company reportedly generates more than US$1 billion in worldwide sales every year.

4. Company: Netflix (Industry: DVD rentals)

Netflix is the world's largest online subscription service for movies, television programming, and other filmed
entertainment rentals. Operating almost like a mail-order
business, the company had evolved a successful and proven
marketing strategy, which helped it to grow into a highly
profitable and established company. The company provides
a monthly flat-fee service for the rental of DVD movies.
A subscriber creates a rank-ordered list, called a rental
queue, of DVDs to rent. The DVDs are delivered individu-
ally via the U.S. Postal Service from an array of regional
warehouses. A subscriber can keep a rented DVD as long as
desired but has a limit on the number of DVDs (determined
by subscription level) that can be checked out at any one
time. To rent a new DVD, the subscriber mails the previ-
ous one back to Netflix in a prepaid mailing envelope.
Upon receipt of the disc, Netflix ships the next disc in
the subscriber's rental queue. The business model is now
coming under threat with the advent of movie downloads,
and analysts are skeptical about the continued success of
Netflix. Netflix itself was to announce its own download
venture in 2007.

5. Company: CavinKare (Industry: Skin and personal care)

CavinKare is a homegrown FMCG company in
India. Its successful entry into the fairness cream segment
with its brand Fairever was based on the observation that
people in rural India drank saffron mixed with milk for a
fairer complexion. The company created a saffron-and-
milk formulation face cream in low-cost sachets—just
US$0.11 for the smallest 9-gram pack. By the end of
2004, just twenty-four months after launch, the company had achieved an 18.5 percent market share among
fairness creams.

6. Company: Nintendo (Industry: Video games)

   The Wii is the fifth home video game console released by Nintendo in 2006. Nintendo is not trying to beat competitors with better, more advanced processors and the more complicated games that hard-core gamers crave. Instead Nintendo's new console is a stripped-down product that aims to widen the market by pulling in nongamers.

7. Company: Wit Capital (Industry: Investment banking)

   Wit Capital was the world's first Web-based investment bank, founded in 1996 by Andrew Klein. At the beginning, Klein wanted to raise money for his microbrewery. When every venture capitalist he could reach rejected his business plan, he went directly to the people. Literally, he launched his IPO via the Internet. In many ways, this was the precursor to Wit Capital's philosophy concerning IPOs. Wit professes a "first-come, first-serve" approach to public offerings, and any Wit customer with at least a $2,000 account is eligible to participate in IPOs. Traditionally, investment banks had given preferential treatment to wealthier customers, with some banks requiring as much as $1 million in an individual account before a customer gets access to IPOs. While the public offering process still isn't completely democratic, Wit's strategy has given investors access to hot IPOs they normally couldn't touch. Wit led online investments in IPOs until it was acquired by E-Trade.

8. Company: Branders.com (Industry: Promotional products)

   Historically, promotional products have been sold by individual salespeople who cover a specified territory and function almost like independent contractors. With the Internet boom at its height, Branders.com hit upon the idea of allowing customers to interact with the company via the Internet rather than through a corps of salespeople.

9. Company: easyCar (Industry: Car rental)

   In April 2000 the easyGroup set up the car rental company easyRentacar (later renamed easyCar), with the only rental car available being the Mercedes-Benz A-Class. The car rental business, which suffered from financial losses and a reputation for poor service, has since closed, but easyCar continues operating as a car rental company via the Internet. It is now profitable and operates in more than sixty countries and more than two thousand locations, selling a full fleet of vehicles. It attempts to be the absolute lowest-cost producer in the car rental business.

10. Company: UTStarcom (Industry: Wireless equipment)

UTStarcom, a California-based wireless communications equipment provider, enables companies to provide a revolutionary wireless service in China called *Xiaolingtong,* or "Little Smart." The service is based on the Internet Protocol (IP) standard and functions like an extended cordless phone. Customers can make and receive wireless calls as long as they don't roam outside a citywide calling area. The solution, also known as "wireless local loop," is cheap to install as well as economical to run, and has found a booming market among individuals who can't afford the cost of cell service or who don't need extended area calling. Consumers with Wi-Fi access in their home can replace their traditional home phone with the UTStarcom handset and start reaping the benefits of wireless VoIP phone service right away.

11. Company: Redfin (Industry: Real estate agents)

Redfin is a U.S. real estate company that lets you buy and sell MLS-listed homes online. The company claims to be industry's first online real estate brokerage, doing its best to completely remove real estate agents and brokers from at least half of home sales. Redfin combines MLS listing information (homes for sale) with historical sales data (homes already sold) into a single map. If you find a home you like and want to place an offer, Redfin will represent you in the buying process. It reimburses you two-thirds of the buy-side real estate fee directly on closing. It operates in a limited number of markets (Seattle, the San Francisco Bay Area, Southern California, Boston) at this time, but is expanding steadily.

12. Company: ING Direct (Industry: Financial services)

ING Direct, a straight-to-consumer banking service with a highly focused product line, is a branchless direct bank with operations in Austria, Australia, Canada, France, Germany, Italy, Spain, the United Kingdom, and the United States. ING Direct is part of the ING Group. It offers services over the Internet, by phone, or by mail. It has attracted customers by offering high-interest savings accounts, no service charges, and no minimum account balance requirements.

13. Company: Line 6 (Industry: Electric guitars)

A U.S.-based company founded in 1996, Line 6 launched an electric guitar, the Variax, which digitally re-creates any of twenty-five vintage guitar sounds at the touch of a knob, allowing you to use the same instrument to perform with a variety of sounds. For guitar players who want to get a range of classic sounds and can't afford to buy a dozen different guitars, it's a compelling offer. Models range in price from under $500 to around $1,500, making them price-competitive with mid-market guitars from Fender and Gibson. Line 6 also offers a lot more fun with computer-based add-ons for additional custom modeling, digital effects, recording, Web-based instruction, and so on.

14. Company: SKY-click (Industry: Call centers)

SKY-click is an innovative call center solution based on Skype, developed by a Swiss start-up company in Geneva. It is a 100 percent Web solution to set up your call center, and very easy to implement and use. The service does not require any particular hardware investment and can be easily integrated in a Web site (for e-commerce, for example).

15. Case: Pay-as-you-go system for road access (Industry: Roads and parking)

      The role of municipal governments with regard to transport is starting to change: after a hundred years of expanding highways and roads with cheap parking so that commuters can gain access to cities, some places like London are trying to keep drivers out by charging a congestion fee per car. Parking meters and roads are among the most fragmented, inconsistent, and unchanged infrastructures in cities today. Applied Location Corp. of Toronto and a few companies including Siemens are working on big changes. ALC is developing a satellite-based pay-as-you-go system for road access, parking, and insurance. The technology is straightforward, but the impact on business models and consumer behavior could be massive.

16. Company: MinuteClinics (Industry: Health care)

      MinuteClinics operates rapid-service walk-in clinics located in such venues as CVS pharmacies, Target stores, and supermarkets. It is based on the premise that certain simple health problems can be more quickly and cheaply diagnosed and treated at a walk-in clinic than in a doctor's office or an emergency room. It employs nurse practitioners armed with software that helps them test for and treat a handful of medical conditions, including bronchitis; ear, eye, and bladder infections; and the flu. The software has the most up-to-date medical guidelines for diagnosis and treatment and applies strict rules that help ensure consistency of service. If patients come in with complaints not on the list or symptoms that indicate something more serious, they are referred to a doctor or an emergency room.

17. Case: Exchange-traded funds (Industry: Mutual funds)

      Exchange-traded funds (or ETFs) are open-ended mutual funds that can be traded at any time throughout the course of the day. Typically, ETFs try to replicate a stock market index such as the S&P 500 or the Hang Seng Index, a market sector such as energy or technology, or a commodity such as gold or petroleum. However, as ETFs proliferated in 2006 from under a hundred in number to almost four hundred by the end of the year, the trend has been away from these simpler index-tracking funds to intellidexes and other proprietary groupings of stocks.

18. Company: Red Hat (Industry: Software and operating systems)

   Red Hat is one of the larger and better-recognized companies dedicated to open source software. It is also the largest distributor of the GNU/Linux operating system. Red Hat was founded in 1993 and has its corporate headquarters in the United States, with satellite offices worldwide. The Linux operating system (OS) when introduced was inferior in performance to other server operating systems like Unix and Windows NT. But the Linux OS distributed through Red Hat is supposed to be inexpensive compared to other server operating systems.

19. Case: Blogs (Industry: Publishing)

   Initially blogs started out as simple tools to let people publish and share ideas on the Web without having to learn html, set up servers, employ Web developers, or deal with network administrators. They were simple, powerful, and cheap. Many of these blogger tools have adapted to the rapidly changing user base by adding new functionality without losing the core simplicity. New products have sprung up in response to the needs of new classes of bloggers who want to be able to create communities, create collaborative writing spaces, and so on.

20. Company: Adobe Apollo (Industry: Software)

   Adobe Flash can be found in 98 percent of all PCs in the world. It brings interactivity out of the browser and into the desktop. It is designed to link online functionalities with advanced client and desktop features and is betting on the idea that there is a lot of demand for dedicated desktop application interfaces to online services that can be "written once, run anywhere." Apollo is a Web service and a Flash Web site, and an architecture unto itself.

Appendix B

HOW TO ENHANCE CORPORATE CREATIVITY*

Chapter Two examined how the fundamental questioning of a company's accepted "Who-What-How" position could be the source of new business-model ideas. There are, however, other ways to enhance corporate creativity. Appendix B.1 describes a number of other tactics that could be used for this purpose, while Appendix B.2 explains why mental models or sacred cows (such as the organization's existing Who-What-How position) are among the biggest obstacles to creativity. Appendix B.3 explores yet another sacred cow—the definition of your business—and describes a way of overcoming it.

B.1 More Ways to Get Creative

Questioning the firm's current Who-What-How position and the business it believes itself to be in is only one way to enhance corporate creativity. Many more tactics exist. For example, another source of business-model innovation is to introduce variety in the thinking process used to develop strategy. New ideas emerge more easily when people manage to escape from a mechanistic way of thinking about an issue and allow their brains to approach the issue from different perspectives or angles. The goal, therefore, is to begin the thinking process at different starting points. For example, instead of thinking: "This is my customer, this is what they want, and this is how I can offer it," it may be useful to start with: "What

---

* Additional commentary for Chapter Two.

are my unique capabilities, what specific needs can I satisfy, and who would be the 'right' customer to approach?"

To develop its business model, a company basically has to decide on three key parameters—the Who, the What, and the How: Who are my customers, what do they want, how can I satisfy these wants? The thinking process could, therefore, go through three stages: Start out by defining who the selected customers will be and then decide on the What and the How; or start the thinking by deciding first what products and services to offer and then decide on the Who and the How; or start with the How and then decide on the Who and the What.

Another useful thought process is to take the accepted definition of the business as given and then try to think of

- New customers or new customer segments
- New customer needs
- New application of core competences

Having come up with a certain number of ideas, a company should revisit the "what is my business" question and—for every new definition that comes to mind—repeat these three steps. Again, the objective is to try to see the business from as many different perspectives as possible in the hope that this will allow managers to see new ways of playing the game.

Another useful way to enhance corporate creativity is to put in place an *organizational environment* that promotes innovative behaviors. The organizational environment of any company is made up of four key ingredients: the measurement and incentive systems of the firm; its culture, values, and norms; its structure and processes; and its people, including their skills, mind-sets, and attitudes. It is the combination of these four elements that creates the firm's organizational environment, which in turn supports and promotes behaviors in the organization. Leaders who want more innovation out of their employees must ask themselves, "What internal organizational environment must I create to elicit the innovative behaviors from all my employees?" Without these four elements firmly established as parts of the organizational environment, innovation will rarely take place.

I cannot emphasize this point strongly enough. Company after company sends executives on courses to help them change their attitudes and behaviors, to make them more innovative or more customer-oriented. What these companies forget is that training does not change people's attitudes or behavior. People will not change what they do because someone else tells them to. They will only change if they have the right incentives and the right culture and values—in short, the right organizational environment.

B.2 What Are Mental Models?

Unquestionably, a prerequisite for business-model innovation is an honest and fundamental questioning of the "mental models" or "industry recipes" that seem to govern the behavior of any individual or organization.[1] A *mental model* is nothing more than a person's beliefs about any issue—be it family or business or the world as a whole. Thus, for example, someone who says, "I think everybody should go to church on Sunday" is simply expressing their mental model on the subject. Some of the other terms that refer to the same thing as a mental model are *rules and regulations, habits, managerial frames, assumptions, mind-sets, paradigms, conventional wisdom, industry recipes, customs,* and *institutional memory.*[2]

Research has shown that every human being has a mental model that develops over time, primarily through education and experience. Similarly, organizations develop mental models—manifested in the organization's culture, routines, and unwritten rules of behavior. Thus it is common to hear statements such as "This is how we do business in this industry," which are nothing more than the expression of an organization's mental model. Organizational mental models, like those of individuals, are developed over time primarily through education and experiences.

Mental models can be beneficial because they make it possible to process information and make decisions quickly. However, very strong mental models can hinder active thinking and the adoption of new ideas, because they act as filters that screen incoming information. As a result, people with very strong mental models tend to hear or see what already supports their existing beliefs and ways of operating, while any new information that does not support what they already believe is generally discarded as "wrong" or "not applicable in our case." It is therefore essential to routinely question your mental models. Questioning does not necessarily mean abandonment—you can certainly question your mental models and decide that nothing's wrong with them. But questioning should allow you to think actively about assumptions you make about your business and about how you behave in that business.

Usually, human beings (and organizations) escape their mental models only after a crisis—this is why it is so easy to find examples of firms that discover new ways of competing in their business only when their backs are against the wall. Outsiders who have different mental models from the ones prevailing in an organization can also act as catalysts in prompting an organization to rethink the way it does business. Thus the entry of a new CEO (especially one who comes from a totally different industry) can kick-start the innovation process. Active benchmarking of outsiders could also allow the active questioning of existing mental models and open people's minds to other possibilities.

Another useful tactic is to develop a questioning attitude that continuously asks why—for example, "Why are we selling our products like this?" When this question is legitimized by, for example, supporting it with descriptions of organizations that are selling their products in a different way and are quite profitable, then the why question can be a powerful wake-up call. Another useful tactic for encouraging people to question their mental models is by actually creating a crisis in the organization. A constructive way of doing this is by giving the organization a new stretch objective to aim for—a strategic intent.[3] Provided you can actually convince the organization that this objective is as worthwhile as it is challenging, people will recognize that it cannot be achieved by doing the same old things better. They'll soon realize that they will have to think and behave differently to achieve such a goal.

A plethora of other tactics can help a company escape its mental models; the list presented here is not meant to be exhaustive.[4] The important thing to note is that business-model innovation will not occur unless the underlying mental models are first questioned.

B.3 How to Redefine Your Business

There is no right or wrong way to define a business. Nor can you know beforehand whether a certain definition will be a winner.[5] The important thing is to ask the question, to think of the implications of a possible redefinition, to assess what new tactics should be adopted if you were to redefine, to think whether your core competences will allow you to carry out these tactics efficiently, and so on. Thus, asking the question is only a trigger to thinking actively.

Looking historically at the issue of how to define a business, I can identify three schools of thought. Traditionally, companies defined their business by the product they were selling. Thus, you had companies who were in the car business (such as Ford), or the airplane business (such as Boeing), or the cigarette business (such as Philip Morris). This way of defining the business came under severe attack in the early 1960s, following Ted Levitt's influential article, "Marketing Myopia."[6] Levitt argued that defining the business by product is too narrow and can lead a company astray. He championed the notion that a company should define its business by the customer function it is trying to fulfill. Thus, he argued,

> The railroads are in trouble today . . . because they let others take customers away from them because they assumed themselves to be in the railroad business rather than in the transportation business. The reason they defined their industry wrong was because they were railroad-oriented instead of transportation-oriented; they were product-oriented instead of customer-oriented.

This way of looking at the business emphasized the importance of customers and encouraged companies to identify the underlying functionality of their products. By asking, "What benefits does the customer derive from my product?" a company could identify its true contribution to the customer, and this would define its business. Thus, instead of thinking of your business as the car business, it is better to think of it as the transport business—or the entertainment business or whatever other function you see your product fulfilling.

Recently, a third perspective has emerged that basically argues that companies must think of their business as a portfolio of core competences.[7] For example, Sony might want to argue that it is in the business of selling "pocketability," or Apple that it is in the business of applying "user-friendliness."

None of these three basic approaches to defining the business is the one correct approach. Each has its merits and each has its limitations. As noted, what is a good definition for one company may be bad for another—it all depends on each company's unique capabilities. The best definition is the one that allows the company to employ its capabilities in the best possible way and thus gain competitive advantage relative to its competitors. What usually kick-starts innovative thinking is not the adoption of any one of these three approaches but rather the continuous switching from one definition to another—and the continuous thinking of the business implications for the company as it switches from one definition to another. The breakthrough usually comes when a company has a dominant way of defining its business (say product-driven) and all of a sudden begins thinking of its business in another way (say customer-driven).

The mental exercise that a company should go through consists of four steps:

1.   First, make a list of all possible definitions of the business. (For example, the list for BMW may look like this: I am in the car business, the prestige car business, the transport business, the ego business, the business of satisfying the transport needs of yuppies, the driving business, the engineering business, the upmarket global car business, and so on.) Make the list as long as possible.

2.   Second, evaluate each definition according to a series of criteria. These are the most pertinent criteria to use: If I define my business as "X," who are my customers and what do they need? Who are my competitors? Can I satisfy these customer needs in a unique (better) way relative to my competitors? Is my definition of the market attractive (that is, growing in the future, protected by barriers, and so on)? What will be the key success factors in this business? Can I deliver? How do my competitors behave and what does that imply as to how they have defined the business? Does this definition allow me to satisfy my personal objectives for this company? The same series of questions should be used to evaluate every possible definition. The goal is to identify the definition that gives your company maximum strength relative to competitors.

3.   Third, choose one definition. This is a crucial step. Making a choice implies certain follow-up decisions. It implies, for example, that the company will invest in certain products or certain country subsidiaries and not in others. It also implies that certain managers will lose out in the next budget round and others will win. As a result of the serious implications that this decision entails, most companies fail to make an explicit decision on the issue.

4. Finally, ask, If my competitors redefined the business, what strategy would they be following? How can I prepare for it?

This is the process that a company should go through in deciding how to define its business. Imagine the power of revisiting these questions every year or every two years—in particular, of asking the follow-up question: "Have any changes taken place that make another definition of the business more attractive to my company?" This is the source of business-model innovation—just when everybody else has settled into a certain accepted definition and is behaving accordingly, you discover a new definition that allows you to start playing the game differently and catch everybody off guard. But again, to discover a new definition you must continuously explore for possible new definitions.

The problem is that very few companies actually decide in an explicit way what business they are in, let alone start thinking how to *redefine* the business. Yet this is the most important element of any strategy. Even the few companies that do go through this exercise in an explicit way generally either fail to take a specific decision when the time comes or, having taken a decision that "This is the business I will be in," fail to revisit this decision, believing that it is something cast in concrete, never to be questioned again.

Appendix C

HOW TO MEASURE RELATEDNESS BETWEEN TWO MARKETS*

Traditional measures provide an incomplete picture of relatedness between two markets. Even though the advantages of the strategy of related diversification are usually cast in terms of the cost and differentiation benefits that arise from the cross-utilization of the firm's underlying assets, the actual measurement of relatedness between two businesses often does not even consider the underlying assets residing in these businesses. Relatedness has traditionally been measured either using an objective index such as the entropy index (based on the SIC classification) or in a subjective way such as Rumelt's diversification categories, which consider businesses related when a common skill, resource, market, or purpose applies to each (Rumelt, 1974, p. 29).

What should be done instead is to explore the strategic importance and relatedness of the underlying strategic assets residing in these businesses. This implies two crucial things:

- The relatedness to focus on is *not* the one between two markets at the aggregate level but the one between the strategic assets in business X and the strategic assets in business Y.
- Simple relatedness between strategic assets is not enough—it must also be *strategic*. In other words, it must be difficult for competitors to acquire or develop.

---

* Additional commentary for Chapter Six.

First of all, what are strategic assets? These are all the things that underpin the cost or differentiation drivers of competitive advantage in a certain market. That is, strategic assets are all the factors that explain why a company has a cost or differentiation advantage over its competitors. These include things such as a firm's reputation, its production capacity, its distribution network, its managerial skills, and its R&D capability. They can all be used to give the firm cost or differentiation advantages over its competitors.

Diversification will be of value if a firm can take a certain strategic asset from one business and apply it in another business. Therefore, this is the appropriate definition of relatedness: *Two markets are related if a strategic asset can be taken from one and used in the other.* This is what most companies do when they try to take advantage of their competences in other markets. However, this only tells half the story.

Suppose that I take a strategic asset from business X and apply it in business Y. Business Y clearly benefits from this transfer, but would I be able to develop a competitive advantage in business Y? Will my diversification into business Y end up as a success? A favorable answer to this question depends on my competitors in business Y being unable to quickly and cheaply get their hands on the same strategic asset I have just transferred. If they can purchase the same asset in the open market or if they can substitute for it with an equally effective asset, my competitive advantage will be short-lived and my diversification will fail. If, on the other hand, my competitors cannot access this asset, then by transferring it into a new business, I have given myself a long-term advantage, and I have created the conditions for successful diversification.

All this implies that even if diversification allows a firm to transfer assets from one business into another, this will not necessarily lead to a long-term advantage. Diversification will create value only when it allows for the transfer of unique assets. Put another way, diversification will enhance performance if it allows a business to obtain preferential access to skills, resources, assets, or competences that cannot be purchased in a competitive market or substituted by some other asset that can be purchased competitively or transferred internally by someone else.

Researchers exploring the implications of the resource-based view of the firm have used the term *strategic assets* to denote skills, resources, assets, or competences that are valuable in this sense. More specifically, the characteristics that define strategic assets are imperfect tradeability, imperfect substitutability, and imperfect imitability. Therefore, to identify opportunities for profitable diversification, measures of relatedness should strive to pinpoint opportunities for sharing these strategic assets between two businesses. It is the sharing of strategic assets that leads to successful diversification—not the sharing of just any asset.

The Right Way to Measure Relatedness

The right way for a company to decide whether two businesses are related is to go through the following process:

1. Identify the strategic assets that underpin competitive advantage in the existing business. Then decide which of these strategic assets will be transferred into the new business.

2. Apply the test of relatedness to the strategic asset proposed for transfer. In other words, ask: "Is this asset of use in the other business?"

3. Apply the test of *strategic* relatedness to this asset. That is, ask: "Is this asset unique in that my competitors will not be able to access it quickly and cheaply?"

Only after the asset has passed both these tests should it be considered a candidate for transfer. Diversification will be successful only if it builds on such strategic assets.

Notes

Introduction

1. S. Davies, P. Geroski, M. Lund, and A. Vlassopoulos, "The Dynamics of Market Leadership in UK Manufacturing Industry, 1979–1986," Centre for Business Strategy, London Business School Working Paper No. 93, 1991; and P. Geroski and S. Toker, "The Turnover of Market Leaders in UK Manufacturing: 1979–1986," mimeo, London Business School, 1993.
2. There is only one major exception to this generalization: in cases when the attacker employs a dramatic technological innovation, seven out of ten market leaders lose out—see the fascinating study by James M. Utterback, *Mastering the Dynamics of Innovation* (Boston: Harvard Business School Press, 1994).

Chapter One

1. A more detailed account of the development of Bright Horizons is provided in Roger Brown, "How We Built a Strong Company in a Weak Industry," *Harvard Business Review*, February 2001, pp. 51–57.
2. Discount brokerage Aufhauser & Co., a former subsidiary of Ameritrade, first offered Internet stock trading in 1994. However, it was not until early 1996 (when companies such as Charles Schwab and E-Trade began offering Internet services)

that online trading experienced dramatic growth, rapidly emerging as a new way of doing business in the industry.

3. "The Internet and Financial Services," Morgan Stanley Dean Witter, Equity Research Division, North America, August 1999, p. 17.

Chapter Two

1. For a complete account, see Siri Schubert, "Building a Better Book Club," *Fortune*, May 14, 2007, pp. B5–B6.

2. Ian C. MacMillan and Rita Gunther McGrath, letter published in *Harvard Business Review*, January–February 1997, pp. 154–156, in response to Michael Porter's article: "What Is Strategy?"

3. Hal Rosenbluth, "Tales from a Nonconformist Company," *Harvard Business Review*, July–August 1991, pp. 26–36. Quoted passages on p. 32 and 26, respectively.

4. Quoted in Charles McCoy, "Entrepreneur Smells Aroma of Success in Coffee Bars," *Wall Street Journal*, January 8, 1993, p. B2.

5. Quoted in Peter Gumbel, "Mass Versus Class," *Fortune*, September 17, 2007, p. 54.

6. Quoted in Charles A. Jaffe, "Moving Fast by Standing Still," *Nation's Business*, October 1991, p. 58.

7. Figures cited in "America's Car-Rental Business: Driven into the Ground," *Economist*, January 20, 1996, pp. 76–79.

8. This point is also raised by Gerard Tellis and Peter Golder in "First to Market, First to Fail? Real Causes of Enduring Market Leadership," *Sloan Management Review*, Winter 1996, pp. 65–75. Their argument is that innovators have a vision of the mass market and actively try to produce quality products at low prices to make them appealing to the mass market. Thus the secret of their success is the fact that they target the mass market and succeed in serving it. Although I agree with the point, my research suggests that the importance of luck, good timing, and external events should not be

underestimated as ingredients in the success of the innovators at picking the right niche at the right time.

9. There is a vast literature on the usefulness as well as the limits of "getting close to the customer." See in particular Stuart Macdonald, "Too Close for Comfort? The Strategic Implications of Getting Close to the Customer," *California Management Review* 37, no. 4 (Summer 1995): 8–27; and Itamar Simonson, "Get Closer to Your Customers by Understanding How They Make Choices," *California Management Review* 35, no. 4 (Summer 1993): 68–84.

10. Described in Kenichi Ohmae, "Getting Back to Strategy," *Harvard Business Review*, November–December 1988, pp. 149–156.

11. Figures cited in "What Makes Yoshio Invent," *Economist*, January 12, 1991, p. 61.

12. Quoted in Thomas Steward, "3M Fights Back," *Fortune*, February 5, 1996, p. 44.

13. For a fuller discussion of this point see: C. Markides and P. Williamson, "Related Diversification, Core Competences and Corporate Performance," *Strategic Management Journal* 15 (Special Issue) (1994): 149–165; and C. Markides and P. Williamson, "Corporate Diversification and Organizational Structure: A Resource-Based View," *Academy of Management Journal* 39, no. 2 (1996): 340–367.

14. See, for example, Gary Hamel and C. K. Prahalad, "Strategic Intent," *Harvard Business Review* 67, no. 3 (1989): 63–76; and James Collins and Jerry Porras, *Built to Last: Successful Habits of Visionary Companies* (New York: HarperBusiness, 1994).

15. Quoted in "Osborne: From Brags to Riches," *Business Week*, February 22, 1982, p. 86.

Chapter Three

1. Further details on Cemex can be found in FC Editor, "CEMEX: This Promise Is Set in Concrete," *Fast Company*, Summer 1999.

2. For a full description of the history and features of ARMS see Eric Berkman, "Enterprise Rent-A-Car Staying Ahead of the Curve with Automated Systems," *CIO Magazine*, February 1, 2002.

3. For an excellent analysis of the Inditex model, see Nicolas Harle and Michael Pich, "Marks & Spencer and Zara: Process Competition in the Textile Apparel Industry," INSEAD Case Study 602–010–1, 2002. See also Pankaj Ghemawat and Jose Luis Nueno, "Zara: Fast Fashion," Harvard Business School Case Study, 9–703–497, April 2003.

4. Jamie Anderson, "IT Adoption Within the UK Construction Industry," London Business School—Atos KPMG Research Study, unpublished working paper, June 2004.

5. Michael Dell, Stockton Lecture at London Business School, September 2002.

6. I wonder whether ARMS, given its widespread acceptance by large insurers, might eventually become the industry standard for processing insurance rentals, just as SABRE has become the reservations standard in the travel industry. The question, of course, is whether Enterprise CEO and Chairman Andy Taylor would ever license the system to his competitors.

Chapter Four

1. See C. M. Christensen, *The Innovator's Dilemma: When New Technologies Cause Great to Fail* (Boston: Harvard Business School Press, 1997). For other supporting voices, see R. Burgelman and L. Sayles, *Inside Corporate Innovation* (New York: Free Press, 1986); and C. Gilbert and J. Bower, "Disruptive Change: When Trying Harder Is Part of the Problem," *Harvard Business Review*, May 2002, pp. 3–8.

2. See J. Day, P. Y. Mang, A. Richter, and J. Roberts, "The Innovative Organization: Why New Ventures Need More Than a Room of Their Own," *McKinsey Quarterly*, no. 2 (2001): 21.

3. See M. Iansiti, F. W. McFarlan, and G. Westerman, "Leveraging the Incumbent's Advantage," *Sloan Management Review* 44, no. 4 (2003): 58.

4. A point also suggested by P. Lawrence and J. Lorsch, *Organization and Environment* (Boston: Harvard Business School Press, 1967).

5. A similar matrix to help managers determine whether a firm should use a heavyweight (or lightweight) team inside or outside the existing organization to manage a different business model can be found in Clayton Christensen and Michael Overdorf, "Meeting the Challenge of Disruptive Change," *Harvard Business Review*, March–April 2000, pp. 67–76. The matrix presented in Figure 4.1 differs from theirs in two important dimensions: First, their model only takes into consideration the importance of conflicts (in values and processes). By contrast, I argue that the decision what to do is determined not only by conflicts but also by the possibility of exploiting synergies between the two markets that the two business models are serving. In this sense, my model builds on the intellectual tradition started by Lawrence and Lorsch. Second, my model takes into consideration time—I argue that (besides the pure separation or integration strategies) under certain circumstances, it may be better to separate the new business model at first and later integrate it into the existing organization, and that still other circumstances might make it desirable to integrate the new business model at the beginning with a view to separating it later.

6. E. Kelly, "Edward Jones and Me," *Fortune*, June 12, 2000, p. 145.

Chapter Five

1. See R. Gulati and J. Garino, "Get the Right Mix of Bricks and Clicks," *Harvard Business Review*, May–June 2000, pp. 107–114.

2. See J. Dutton and S. E. Jackson, "Categorizing Strategic Issues: Links to Organizational Action," *Academy of Management Review* 12, no. 1 (1987): 76–90.

3. The Beer Game is described in more detail in Chapter 3 of Peter Senge, *The Fifth Discipline: The Art and Practice of the Learning Organization* (New York: Currency Doubleday, 1994).

4. An excellent account of how to achieve this can be found in Sumantra Ghoshal and Christopher Bartlett, *The Individualized Corporation* (New York: HarperBusiness, 1997).

Chapter Six

1. See in particular: C. Markides and P. Williamson, "Corporate Diversification and Organizational Structure: A Resource-Based View," *Academy of Management Journal* 39, no. 2 (1996): 340–367; and J. Robins and M. F. Wiersema, "A Resource-Based Approach to the Multibusiness Firm," *Strategic Management Journal* 16, no. 4 (1995): 277–299.

Chapter Seven

1. "K-Mart Has to Open Some New Doors on the Future," *Fortune*, July 1977, p. 144.

2. By *radical innovations* I mean innovations such as the market for PDAs in the 1990s or the PC market in the late 1970s, or the market for television sets in the 1950s. These innovations are considered radical or disruptive for two specific reasons: first, they introduce new products that radically change existing consumer habits and behaviors (what on earth did our ancestors do in the evenings without television!); second, the markets that they create undermine the competences and complementary assets on which existing competitors have built their success.

3. My thesis here is that consolidators focus on price and quality, and this in turn attracts the mass-market consumer.

In *Will and Vision* (2002), Gerard Tellis and Peter Golder propose that consolidators start out with a vision of the mass market and then focus on delivering the price and quality that would satisfy their targeted audience. I believe that both scenarios could play out in reality.

Chapter Eight

1. R. Komisar, "The Business Case for Passion: An Interview with Randy Komisar," *Leader to Leader,* no. 19 (Winter 2001): 22–28.
2. C. Markides and P. Geroski, *Fast Second: How Smart Companies Bypass Radical Innovation to Enter and Dominate New Markets* (San Francisco: Jossey-Bass, 2005).
3. Richard Caves, *Creative Industries: Contracts Between Art and Commerce* (Cambridge, Mass.: Harvard University Press, 2000).

Appendix B

1. A very good discussion of "mental models" and how one can escape them is found in J. C. Spender, *Industry Recipes* (Oxford: Basil Blackwell, 1990); and in Peter Grinyer and Peter McKiernan, "Triggering Major and Sustained Changes in Stagnating Companies," in Herman Daems and Howard Thomas (eds.), *Strategic Groups, Strategic Moves and Performance* (New York: Elsevier Science, 1994). A very practical discussion of these issues is found in Joel Arthur Barker, *Paradigms: The Business of Discovering the Future* (New York: HarperCollins, 1992).
2. A survey of just the academic literature has identified eighty-one words that have been used to describe the same thing. See James Walsh, "Managerial and Organizational Cognition: Notes from a Trip Down Memory Lane," *Organization Science* 6, no. 3 (1995): 280–321.

3. See Gary Hamel and C. K. Prahalad, "Strategic Intent," *Harvard Business Review* 67, no. 3 (1989): 63–76.

4. Other tactics one can use to question mental models include monitoring the company's *strategic* health as opposed to its *financial* health, experimenting with new ideas, benchmarking, asking the "What if—" question, monitoring maverick competitors as well as new entrants, talking with noncustomers, bringing in outsiders, institutionalizing a questioning culture, and developing the right incentives.

5. The whole purpose of redefining the business is to identify a specific definition that allows you to maximize the impact of your unique capabilities relative to those of your competitors. Thus what is a good definition for your company may be totally inappropriate for another company, and what is a good definition for your competitor—given its particular strengths—may be totally inappropriate for you. So what makes a definition "good" is in the eyes of the beholder! However, even if you can find a good definition for your company, you just enhance your chances of success. This does not mean that you are guaranteed success!

6. Theodore Levitt, "Marketing Myopia," *Harvard Business Review*, July–August 1960, pp. 138–149.

7. Gary Hamel and C. K. Prahalad, *Competing for the Future* (Boston: Harvard Business School Press, 1994), p. 83; and C. K. Prahalad and Gary Hamel, "The Core Competence of the Corporation," *Harvard Business Review*, May–June 1990, pp. 79–91.

References

Abell, D. *Defining the Business: The Starting Point of Strategic Planning.* Upper Saddle River, N.J.: Prentice Hall, 1980.

"America's Car-Rental Business: Driven into the Ground." *Economist*, Jan. 20, 1996, pp. 76–79.

Anderson, J. "IT Adoption Within the UK Construction Industry." London Business School—Atos KPMG Research Study, unpublished working paper, June 2004.

Anderson, J., and Markides, C. "Creativity Is Not Enough: ICT-Enabled Strategic Innovation."*European Journal of Innovation Management*, 2006, 9(2), 129–148.

Barker, J. A. *Paradigms: The Business of Discovering the Future.* New York: HarperCollins, 1992.

Barney, J. *Gaining and Sustaining Competitive Advantage* (3rd ed.). Upper Saddle River, N.J.: Prentice Hall, 2006.

Bartlett, C., and Ghoshal, S. *Managing Across Borders: The Transnational Solution.* Boston: Harvard Business School Press, 1989.

Berkman, E. "Enterprise Rent-A-Car Staying Ahead of the Curve with Automated Systems," *CIO Magazine*, Feb. 1, 2002.

Birkinshaw, J., and Gibson, C. "Building Ambidexterity into an Organization." *Sloan Management Review*, 2004, 45(4), 47–55.

Bower, J., and Christensen, C. "Disruptive Technologies: Catching the Wave." *Harvard Business Review*, Jan.–Feb. 1995, pp. 43–53.

Brown, R. "How We Built a Strong Company in a Weak Industry." *Harvard Business Review*, Feb. 2001, pp. 51–57.

Bryce, D. J., and Dyer, J. H. "Strategies to Crack Well-Guarded Markets." *Harvard Business Review*, May 2007, pp. 84–92.

Burgelman, R., and Sayles, L. *Inside Corporate Innovation.* New York: Free Press, 1986.

Burns, T., and Stalker, G. M. *The Management of Innovation.* Oxford: Oxford University Press, 1961.

Casadesus-Masanell, R., and Ricart, J. E. "Competing Through Business Models." Harvard Business School, unpublished working paper, June 2007.

Caves, R. *Creative Industries: Contracts Between Art and Commerce.* Cambridge, Mass.: Harvard University Press, 2000.

Charitou, C. "The Response of Established Firms to Disruptive Strategic Innovation: Empirical Evidence from Europe and North America." London Business School, unpublished doctoral dissertation, July 2001.

Charitou, C., and Markides, C. "Responses to Disruptive Strategic Innovation." *Sloan Management Review,* 2003, 44(2), 55–63.

Chen, M-J., and Hambrick, D. C. "Speed, Stealth, and Selective Attack: How Small Firms Differ from Large Firms in Competitive Behavior." *Academy of Management Journal,* 1995, 38(2), 453–482.

Chen, M-J., and MacMillan, I. C. "Nonresponse and Delayed Response to Competitive Moves: The Roles of Competitor Dependence and Action Irreversibility." *Academy of Management Journal,* 1992, 35(3), 539–570.

Chen, M-J., and Miller, D. "Competitive Attack, Retaliation and Performance: An Expectancy-Valence Framework." *Strategic Management Journal,* 1994, 15, 85–102.

Chen, M-J., Smith, K. G., and Grimm, C. M. "Action Characteristics as Predictors of Competitive Responses." *Management Science,* 1992, 38(3), 439–455.

Christensen, C. *The Innovator's Dilemma: When New Technologies Cause Great Firms to Fail.* Boston: Harvard Business School Press, 1997.

Christensen, C., and Overdorf, M. "Meeting the Challenge of Disruptive Change." *Harvard Business Review,* Mar.–Apr. 2000, pp. 67–76.

Christensen, C., and Raynor, M. *The Innovator's Solution.* Boston: Harvard Business School Press, 2003.

Collins, J. *Good to Great.* London: Random House, 2001.

Collins, J., and Porras, J. *Built to Last: Successful Habits of Visionary Companies.* New York: HarperBusiness, 1994.

Cooper, A. C., and Smith, C. G. "How Established Firms Respond to Threatening Technologies." *Academy of Management Executive,* 1992, 6, 55–70.

Danneels, E. "Disruptive Technology Reconsidered: A Critique and Research Agenda." *Journal of Product Innovation Management,* 2004, 21, 246–258.

D'Aveni, R. *Hypercompetition: Managing the Dynamics of Strategic Maneuvering.* New York: Free Press, 1994.

Davies, S., Geroski, P., Lund, M., and Vlassopoulos, A. "The Dynamics of Market Leadership in UK Manufacturing Industry, 1979–1986." Centre for Business Strategy, London Business School Working Paper No. 93, 1991.

Day, J., Mang, P. Y., Richter, A., and Roberts, J. "The Innovative Organization: Why New Ventures Need More Than a Room of Their Own." *McKinsey Quarterly,* 2001, 2, 21.

Dutton, J., and Jackson, S. E. "Categorizing Strategic Issues: Links to Organizational Action." *Academy of Management Review*, 1987, *12*(1), 76–90.

FC Editor, "CEMEX: This Promise Is Set in Concrete." *Fast Company*, Summer 1999.

Geroski, P., and Toker, S. "The Turnover of Market Leaders in UK Manufacturing: 1979–1986." mimeo, London Business School, 1993.

Ghemawat, P., and Nueno, J. L. "Zara: Fast Fashion." Harvard Business School Case Study, 9–703–497, Apr. 2003.

Ghoshal, S., and Bartlett, C. *The Individualized Corporation.* New York: HarperBusiness, 1997.

Ghoshal, S., and Gratton, L. "Integrating the Enterprise." *Sloan Management Review*, 2003, *44*(1), 31–38.

Gilbert, C. "The Disruption Opportunity." *Sloan Management Review*, 2003, *44*(4), 27–32.

Gilbert, C., and Bower, J. "Disruptive Change: When Trying Harder Is Part of the Problem." *Harvard Business Review*, May 2002, pp. 3–8.

Govindarajan, V., and Trimble, C. "Building Breakthrough Businesses Within Established Organizations." *Harvard Business Review*, 2005a, *83*(5), 58–68.

Govindarajan, V., and Trimble, C. *Ten Rules for Strategic Innovators: From Idea to Execution.* Boston: Harvard Business School Press, 2005b.

Grant, R. *Contemporary Strategy Analysis* (6th ed.). London: Blackwell, 2007.

Grinyer, P., and McKiernan, P. "Triggering Major and Sustained Changes in Stagnating Companies." In Herman Daems and Howard Thomas (eds.), *Strategic Groups, Strategic Moves and Performance.* New York: Elsevier Science, 1994.

Gulati, R., and Garino, J. "Get the Right Mix of Bricks and Clicks." *Harvard Business Review*, May-June 2000, pp. 107–114.

Gumbel, P. "Mass Versus Class." *Fortune*, Sept. 17, 2007, pp. 53–56.

Hambrick, D. C., and Fredrickson, J. W. "Are You Sure You Have a Strategy?" *Academy of Management Executive*, 2001, *15*(4), 48–59.

Hamel, G. "Strategy as Revolution." *Harvard Business Review*, July-Aug. 1996, pp. 69–82.

Hamel, G. "Bringing Silicon Valley Inside." *Harvard Business Review*, Sept.-Oct. 1999, pp. 71–84.

Hamel, G. *Leading the Revolution.* Boston: Harvard Business School Press, 2000.

Hamel, G., and Prahalad, C. K. "Strategic Intent." *Harvard Business Review*, 1989, *67*(3), 63–76.

Hamel, G., and Prahalad, C. K. "Corporate Imagination and Expeditionary Marketing." *Harvard Business Review*, 1991, *69*(4), 81–92.

Hamel, G., and Prahalad, C. K. *Competing for the Future.* Boston: Harvard Business School Press, 1994.

Hammer, M. "Deep Change: How Operational Innovation Can Transform Your Company." *Harvard Business Review*, Apr. 2004, pp. 84–93.

Harle, N., and Pich, M. "Marks & Spencer and Zara: Process Competition in the Textile Apparel Industry." INSEAD Case Study 602–010–1, 2002.

Harreld, B. "Which Businesses to Grow? Which Not?" *Across the Board*, Nov.-Dec. 2004, pp. 9–10.

Iansiti, M., McFarlan, F. W., and Westerman, G. "Leveraging the Incumbent's Advantage." *Sloan Management Review*, 2003, 44(4), 58–65.

"The Internet and Financial Services" (white paper). New York: Morgan Stanley Dean Witter, Equity Research Division, Aug. 1999.

Jaffe, C. A. "Moving Fast by Standing Still." *Nation's Business*, Oct. 1991, p. 58.

Johnson, M., and Suskewicz, J. "Business Model Innovation." *Strategy & Innovation*, 2007, 5(4), 37.

Kelly, E. "Edward Jones and Me." *Fortune*, June 12, 2000, p. 145.

Kim, C. W., and Mauborgne, R. "Value Innovation: The Strategic Logic of High Growth." *Harvard Business Review*, Jan.-Feb. 1997, pp. 103–112.

Kim, C. W., and Mauborgne, R. "Creating New Market Space." *Harvard Business Review*, Jan.–Feb. 1999, pp. 83–93.

Kim, C. W., and Mauborgne, R. *Blue Ocean Strategy: How to Create Uncontested Market Space and Make the Competition Irrelevant.* Boston: Harvard Business School Press, 2005.

"K-Mart Has to Open Some New Doors on the Future." *Fortune*, July 1977, p. 144.

Komisar, R. "The Business Case for Passion: An Interview with Randy Komisar." *Leader to Leader*, Winter 2001, 19, 22–28.

Kuhn, J., and Marsick, V. "Action Learning for Strategic Innovation in Mature Organizations." *Action Learning: Research and Practice*, 2005, 2(1), 29–50.

Lawrence, P., and Lorsch, J. *Organization and Environment.* Boston: Harvard Business School Press, 1967.

Levitt, T. "Marketing Myopia." *Harvard Business Review*, July-Aug. 1960, pp. 138–149.

Macdonald, S. "Too Close for Comfort? The Strategic Implications of Getting Close to the Customer." *California Management Review*, 1995, 37(4), 8–27.

MacMillan, I. C., and McGrath, R. G. Letter responding to Michael Porter's article, "What Is Strategy?" *Harvard Business Review*, Jan.–Feb. 1997, pp. 154–156.

Markides, C. "Strategic Innovation." *Sloan Management Review*, 1997, 38(3), 9–23.

Markides, C. "Strategic Innovation in Established Companies." *Sloan Management Review*, 1998, 39(3), 31–42.

Markides, C. *All the Right Moves: A Guide to Crafting Breakthrough Strategy.* Boston: Harvard Business School Press, 2000.

Markides, C., and Charitou, C. "Competing with Dual Business Models: A Contingency Approach." *Academy of Management Executive,* 2004, *18*(3), 22–36.

Markides, C., and Geroski, P. *Fast Second: How Smart Companies Bypass Radical Innovation to Enter and Dominate New Markets.* San Francisco: Jossey-Bass, 2005.

Markides, C., and Williamson, P. "Related Diversification, Core Competences and Corporate Performance." *Strategic Management Journal,* 1994, *15* (Special Issue), 149–165.

Markides, C., and Williamson, P. "Corporate Diversification and Organizational Structure: A Resource-Based View." *Academy of Management Journal,* 1996, *39*(2), 340–367.

McCoy, C. "Entrepreneur Smells Aroma of Success in Coffee Bars." *Wall Street Journal,* Jan. 8, 1993, p. B2.

McGrath, R. G., and MacMillan, I. *The Entrepreneurial Mindset.* Boston: Harvard Business School Press, 2000.

Mitchell, D., and Coles, C. *The Ultimate Competitive Advantage: Secrets of Continually Developing a More Profitable Business Model.* San Francisco: Berrett-Koehler, 2003.

Ohmae, K. "Getting Back to Strategy." *Harvard Business Review,* Nov.-Dec. 1988, pp. 149–156.

O'Reilly, C., III, and Tushman, M. "The Ambidextrous Organization." *Harvard Business Review,* 2004, *82*(4), 74–81.

"Osborne: From Brags to Riches." *Business Week,* Feb. 22, 1982, p. 86.

Porter, M. E. *Competitive Strategy.* New York: Free Press, 1980.

Porter, M. E. *Competitive Advantage.* New York: Free Press, 1985.

Porter, M. E. "What Is Strategy?" *Harvard Business Review,* Nov.–Dec. 1996, pp. 61–78.

Prahalad, C. K., and Hamel, G. "The Core Competence of the Corporation." *Harvard Business Review,* May–June 1990, pp. 79–91.

Robins, J., and Wiersema, M. F. "A Resource-Based Approach to the Multibusiness Firm." *Strategic Management Journal,* 1995, *16*(4), 277–299.

Rosenblum, D., Tomlinson, D., and Scott, L. "Bottom-Feeding for Blockbluster Businesses." *Harvard Business Review,* Mar. 2003, pp. 52–59.

Rosenbluth, H. "Tales from a Nonconformist Company." *Harvard Business Review,* July–Aug. 1991, pp. 26–36.

Rumelt, R. *Strategy, Structure and Economic Performance.* Cambridge, Mass.: Division of Research, Graduate School of Business Administration, Harvard University, 1974.

Schnaars, S. P. *Managing Imitation Strategies.* New York: Free Press, 1994.

Schubert, S. "Building a Better Book Club." *Fortune*, May 14, 2007, pp. B5–B6.

Senge, P. *The Fifth Discipline: The Art and Practice of the Learning Organization.* New York: Currency Doubleday, 1994.

Simonson, I. "Get Closer to Your Customers by Understanding How They Make Choices." *California Management Review*, 1993, *35*(4), 68–84.

Slywotzky, A. J. *Value Migration: How to Think Several Moves Ahead of the Competition.* Boston: Harvard Business School Press, 1996.

Slywotzky, A. J., and Morrison, M. *The Profit Zone.* New York: Three Rivers Press, 2002.

Smith, K. G., Grimm, C. M., Chen, M-J., and Gannon, M. J. "Predictors of Competitive Strategic Actions: Theory and Preliminary Evidence." *Journal of Business Research*, 1989, *18*, 245–258.

Spender, J. C. *Industry Recipes.* Oxford: Basil Blackwell, 1990.

Stalk, G., Jr., Pecaut, D., and Burnett, B. "Breaking Compromises, Breakaway Growth." *Harvard Business Review*, Sept.–Oct. 1996, pp. 131–139.

Steward, T. "3M Fights Back." *Fortune*, Feb. 5, 1996, p. 44.

Tellis, G., and Golder, P. "First to Market, First to Fail? Real Causes of Enduring Market Leadership." *Sloan Management Review*, Winter 1996, pp. 65–75.

Tellis, G., and Golder, P. *Will and Vision: How Latecomers Grow to Dominate Markets.* New York: McGraw-Hill, 2002.

Tushman, M. L., and O'Reilly, C. A., III. "Ambidextrous Organizations: Managing Evolutionary and Revolutionary Change." *California Management Review*, 1996, *38*(4), 8–30.

Utterback, J. M. *Mastering the Dynamics of Innovation.* Boston: Harvard Business School Press, 1994.

Voelpel, S., Leibold, M., Tekie, E., and Von Krogh, G. "Escaping the Red Queen Effect in Competitive Strategy." *European Management Journal*, 2005, *23*(1), 37–49.

Walsh, J. "Managerial and Organizational Cognition: Notes from a Trip Down Memory Lane." *Organization Science*, 1995, *6*(3), 280–321.

"What Makes Yoshio Invent." *Economist*, Jan. 12, 1991, p. 61.

Acknowledgments

In 1997 I published an article titled "Strategic Innovation" in *Sloan Management Review*. The ideas in that article were the product of a two-year study on companies that strategically innovated in their industries and had evolved in my mind as a result of debates and advice from the remarkable set of colleagues at London Business School whom I have been privileged to work with. In particular, I'd like to single out my late colleague, Professor Sumantra Ghoshal. Sumantra protected and challenged me through the early years of my academic career and in return I stole his ideas! For this, I am eternally grateful.

The ideas in that article ten years ago proved to be the intellectual seeds of this book. They first gave birth to my MBA course on strategic innovation and then led to a series of published articles, exploring various aspects of the phenomenon. This book is simply an attempt to collect and organize these ideas into a coherent thesis. I gratefully acknowledge the feedback and comments of my colleagues here at London Business School and thank the numerous executive and MBA students who have been subjected to lectures and debates on the issues raised in the book. I would especially like to thank my PhD student Constantinos Charitou, who actually carried out a lot of the research reported in this book, and who coauthored with me much of what appears in Chapter Six.

Several people have read earlier versions of the book and provided constructive feedback. I first thank my brothers, George and Angelos, as well as my sister, Maria, who have been the harshest critics of the ideas presented here. I also thank Daniel Oyon,

Freek Vermeulen, Charis Charalambous, Savvakis Savvides, and Patrick Raming, whose comments led to several revisions of the text. And of course Sharon Wilson, who has been a constant source of support and advice through the years!

A portion of the research summarized here has already been reported in academic and managerial journals. Much in Chapter Two is based on material that appeared in highly condensed form in *Sloan Management Review*, Vol. 38, No. 3, Spring 1997, pp. 9–23. Chapter Four is reprinted from the *European Journal of Innovation Management*, Vol. 9, No. 2 (2006), pp. 129–148. Chapters Four and Five are based on research that was originally reported in *Academy of Management Executive*, Vol. 18, No. 3, August 2004, pp. 22–36. Finally, Chapter Six was originally published in *Sloan Management Review*, Winter 2003, Vol. 44, No. 2, pp. 55–63. I am grateful to the several publishers who have granted their permission for me to elaborate and integrate these materials in this book.

This book was supposed to be a joint effort with my late colleague Paul Geroski. His untimely death means that I cannot have him as my coauthor on yet another book project, and I am poorer for that. I dedicate this book to his memory.

The Author

Constantinos Markides is Professor of strategic and international management and holds the Robert P. Bauman Chair of Strategic Leadership at the London Business School (LBS). He is also chairman of the Strategic and International Management Department at LBS. A native of Cyprus, he received his BA (Distinction) and MA in economics from Boston University, and his MBA and DBA from the Harvard Business School. He has worked as an associate with the Cyprus Development Bank and as a research associate at the Harvard Business School.

He has done research and published on the topics of strategic innovation, corporate restructuring, refocusing, and international acquisitions. His first book, *Diversification, Refocusing and Economic Performance*, was published by MIT Press in December 1995. His second book, *All the Right Moves: A Guide to Crafting Breakthrough Strategy*, was published by Harvard Business School Press in 2000 and was short-listed for the Igor Ansoff Strategic Management Award 2000. A third book, coedited with Michael Cusumano and titled *Strategic Thinking for the Next Economy*, was published by Jossey-Bass in May 2001. His next book (with Paul Geroski), titled *Fast Second: How Smart Companies Bypass Radical Innovation to Enter and Dominate New Markets*, was published in January 2005 by Jossey-Bass and was on the Short List of the Financial Times–Goldman Sachs Management Book of the Year in 2005.

His publications have also appeared in journals such as the *Harvard Business Review, Sloan Management Review, Directors & Boards, Leader to Leader, Long Range Planning, Business Strategy Review, British Journal of Management, Journal of International*

Business Studies, *Strategic Management Journal*, and the *Academy of Management Journal.*

He has taught in many in-company executive education programs and is on the Academic Board of the Cyprus International Institute of Management. He is the associate editor of the *European Management Journal* and is on the editorial boards of the *Strategic Management Journal*, the *Academy of Management Journal*, the *Journal of Management and Governance*, and the *Sloan Management Review*. He is a member of the Academy of Management and the Strategic Management Society and was a fellow of the World Economic Forum in Davos, Switzerland, 1999–2003. His current research interests include the management of diversified firms and the use of innovation and creativity to achieve strategic breakthroughs.

Index

Intel, 100
Internet: blogs, 182; Cisco's model and, 72–75; ING Direct on, 25–26, 180; online trading models for, 90–91. *See also* Online brokerage market
IRVs (immediate response vehicles), 60

J

J. C. Penney Company, 145
Johnson & Johnson, 157, 159
Johnson, M., 4–5
Jones, Ted, 59

K

K-Mart, 41, 52, 143–144, 145
Kelleher, Herb, 35
Kim, C. W., xii, 23, 24
Kingfisher Airlines, 175
Klein, Andrew, 178
KLM, 86, 100
Kodak, 146, 147–149
Komisar, Randy, 170
Kresge Co., 41, 143–144
Kuhn, J., xiii

L

Lan & Spar Bank, 86, 92–93, 100, 144–145
Lansley, Nick, 94–95
Lawrence, P., 101–102
Leclerc, Eduard, 117
Leibold, M., 4
Leica, 154, 156
Lerner, Sandy, 72
Lever Bros., 145–146
Lexus, 100
Library Thing, 24–25
Line 6, 180
London Business School, ix
Lorsch, J., 101–102

M

MacMillan, I., 24
Management: choosing managers for new units, 102–103; creating stretch goals, 47–49; deciding how to operate dual models, 111–115; questions to direct innovation, 21–22, 53; supporting innovation, 166–168;

treating new models as opportunities, 105–108, 120
Management of Innovation, The (Burns and Stalker), 170
Managing dual business models, 86–96; exploiting synergy with separation strategy, 101–104, 120; failures of separation strategies, 100–101; integration strategies for, 87, 90–91, 97; phased integration strategies for, 87, 91–93, 97; phased separation strategies, 87, 93–96, 97; variables influencing strategies, 87
Mang, P.Y., 114
Markets: attacking existing leaders in, 150–151; attributes of disruptive innovation and traditional, 11–13; created through innovation, xx–xxi; discovering and scaling up niche, 151–153, 154; entering into established, 145–151; examining mental models of, 28–31, 187–189; innovation enlarging, 6–7; measuring relatedness of, 193–195; protecting new, 70–75; redefining, 28–31; shifting basis of competition, 154–162; strategic relatedness of, 129–130. *See also* Online brokerage market
Markides, C., xiii, 4, 18, 24, 55, 114
Marsick, V., xiii
Mason, Linda, 1
Mason, Roger, 1
Mattel, 27
Mauborgne, R., xii, 23, 24
McFarlan, F. W., 114
McGrath, R. G., 24
McMillan, I. C., 138
Medco Containment Services, 150
Mental models, 28–31, 187–189
Merrill Lynch, 38, 91, 105
Middleton, David, 99–100
Migrating to new models, 136–138, 140, 141, 143–145, 162
Miller, D., 138
Mills, Victor, 158
MinuteClinics, xi–xii, 181
Mitchell, D., xiii, 4, 5
Morgan Stanley Dean Witter, 9
Morrison, M., 4, 5

Rosenbluth Travel, 29–30
Rumelt, R., 193
Ryanair, 4, 121

S

Sara Lee, 27, 50–51
Sari-Sari stores, 66, 67, 68
Saturn Motor Company, 85
Scaling up markets: established firms
    and, 153–162; examples of,
    151–153; migrating and, 136–138,
    140, 141; quick response time for,
    70–75
Schnaars, S. P., 138
Schou, Peter, 92, 144
Schultz, Howard, 30, 146
Schumpeter, Joseph, 152
Scott, L., 57, 60
Security APL Inc., 136
Seiko, 38, 108, 130–131
Separation strategy, 87–90, 97;
    disruptive innovation and,
    xvii–xviii; examples of, 89–90;
    exploiting synergies for ambidexterity,
    101–104, 120; failures of, 99–100;
    going beyond separate units,
    113–114; illustrated, 87; management
    tips when using, 111–112; research
    on, 84–85
Sincronización Dinámica de Operaciones
    (SDO), 62, 79
Singapore Airlines, 88, 100
SKY-click, 180
Slywotzky, A.J., xiii, 4, 5, 7–8, 24
Smart car, 3
Smart Communications, 64–69
Smart Load, 66–68
SMH, 100, 107, 108–109
Smith, C. G., 84
Smith, K. G., 138–139
Sony, 137, 155
Southwest Airlines, 27, 35, 52,
    121, 150
Spalding, Tim, 24–25
Stalk, Jr., G., 24
Stalker, G. M., 170
Starbucks, 27, 30, 146
Start-up firms: attacking existing
    markets, 150–151; business model
    innovations for, xiii, 81, 162
Sterman, John, 115
Strategic assets, 194–195

Strategic decisions: redefining customers,
    31–37; responding to business
    redefinition, 192; reviewing choice of
    products and services, 37–42
Strategic innovations, 18
Strategic relatedness of markets,
    129–130, 193–195
Stretch goals: creating, 47–49, 54;
    examples of setting, 50–51;
    illustrated, 48
Suskewicz, J., 208
Sustaining innovation, 163
Swatch, 7, 27, 100, 107, 108–109,
    110, 131

T

Technology: disruptive innovation of,
    xv–xvi; driving value with, 75–80;
    innovating for economic feasibility,
    77–78; promoting as means for
    innovation, 78–79; scaling up in,
    136–137. *See also* ICT
Tekie, E., 4
Tellis, G., 138
Tesco Direct, 4, 94–96
Texas Instruments, 146, 156
3M, 43, 53, 164–165
Timex, 38, 108, 130–131
Tomlinson, D., 57, 60
Toyota, 100
Tradeoffs adapting innovations, 15–18,
    81–85, 97
Trimble, C., 113, 114
Tushman, M. L., 85, 113, 114

U

Unilever, 65, 66, 145
University of Phoenix, 11, 39
US Steel, 39
USA Today, 146
UTStarcom, 179
Utterback, J. M., 84–85

V

Value chains, 57, 64–70
Value propositions: creating innovative
    ICT, 57; driving value with
    technology, 75–80; examples of new,
    61–64; finding, 39–41; innovations
    with product, 38–39; investing in
    own, 123–127, 140